Cravings

Cravings

A Catholic Wrestles with Food,
Self-Image, and God

Mary DeTurris Poust

ave maria press AmP notre dame, indiana

© 2012 by Mary DeTurris Poust

Founded in 1865, Ave Maria Press is a ministry of the United States Province of Holy Cross.

www.avemariapress.com

Paperback: ISBN-10 1-59471-305-7   ISBN-13 978-1-59471-305-7

E-book: ISBN-10 1-59471-353-7   ISBN-13 978-1-59471-353-8

Cover and text design by Andy Wagoner.

Printed and bound in the United States of America.

Library of Congress Cataloging-in-Publication Data

For my grandmother,

Helen DeJurris,

the strongest and wisest woman I know.

Contents

Acknowledgments

Talking honestly about food issues and self-image isn't always easy, and so I want to start by thanking all those people who opened their hearts and shared their stories so that others might benefit. I was honored to talk to so many wonderful people about their journeys through diet plans and self-esteem struggles to a place of wholeness. Thank you from the bottom of my heart for agreeing to be part of this book.

I also want to thank Bob Hamma, my editor at Ave Maria Press. He was the one who originally suggested I tackle this topic, and, to be honest, I balked at first. Then I began doing some research, and little by little I realized I had a story to tell. Since that time, Bob has treated this book as if it were his own, and I am so grateful that my work has had a champion, a protector, and a fabulous editor as it moved through the various stages of production. Thank you to Susanna Cover for her thorough and thoughtful editing of my manuscript and to everyone at Ave Maria Press who helped make this book a reality, especially Tom Grady and Amanda Williams.

While I was weighing the consequences of poor self-image and food obsessions, my family was patiently waiting for dinners that were later than usual, play dates that were postponed, and an end to the general insanity that typically ensues whenever I write a book. Thank you to my husband, Dennis, who is not only my partner in all things but my personal editor as well. You are the best; I couldn't do any of this without you. And thank you to our beautiful children, Noah, Olivia, and Chiara, who always find a way to counter my busyness with steady doses of love, laughter, and handmade drawings that hang beside me as I work.

Finally, I want to thank the family members and friends whose prayers quietly sustained me throughout this process. Whenever I was losing ground or feeling overwhelmed, I took comfort in the knowledge that your whispered prayers, unheard and unseen by others, were keeping me on track and moving me forward.

This book was an unexpected gift, one that unfolded before me as I explored the depths of my heart. I felt the Spirit at work as I wrote my way through issues and subjects that were sometimes difficult to address. It is in weakness that we are made strong, St. Paul reminds us. I hope that by sharing my moments of weakness with you, we can both find strength in the only One who makes us whole and complete.

Prologue

Food—and our relationship with it—has gotten a bad rap right from the very beginning. What chance did it have when the whole of humanity's downfall hung on one bite of the wrong food? Talk about eating issues.

The connection between food and faith certainly doesn't end there. The apple in the Garden of Eden was really just a crudité in the endless banquet that is our spiritual story. Throughout both the Old and New Testaments, we can trace a faith history that is marked by fasting and feasting, culminating in the ultimate feast, the Eucharist.

For Catholics, any conversation about the food-faith connection will always come back around to this one central theme. Ours is a faith centered on a meal. Day after day, week after week, we gather around a table to break bread with our spiritual family in much the same way we gather around the dinner table with our individual families each night.

As we begin to explore the undeniable connection between spiritual nourishment and physical nourishment, we will constantly look toward the Eucharist, toward Christ, as our grounding point, our center in the storm of food obsession, weight gain and loss, and plain old low self-esteem.

If you simply want to explore food and spirituality, there are plenty of books out there to help you do that. But if you want to get to the heart of the matter—your relationship with God and your ability to become the person you were created to be, unfettered by food-related problems—you'll need to go places those other books can't take you. And that's where this book will help, where this book is different.

From the very beginning, even from the selection of its title—*Cravings: A Catholic Wrestles with Food, Self-Image, and God*—this book has shown itself to be something far more complex and challenging than what's typically served up in books on food and spirituality. My editors and I went back and forth trying to choose just the right words to convey on the cover what readers would find on the pages inside. *Cravings* says it best, because whether you're hungry for food or God, self-acceptance or inner peace, there is a craving at the heart of it. But it goes even deeper than that. Like Jacob wrestling with the angel, we are often our own worst enemies when it comes to working through our issues and learning to rest in God's love.

Cravings is not simply a food-focused book that dabbles in spirituality. It is a Christ-focused book that addresses the food issues that haunt so many of us, whether we are overweight, underweight, or exactly where we're supposed to be. Because sometimes—often—the number on the scale has nothing to do with the depth of the struggle.

The physical hungers that lead to constant snacking and high-calorie meals often mask something much deeper, a spiritual hunger that can never be satisfied by anything we buy at the grocery store or whip up in a food processor. What can satisfy us once and for all? Only God can. So this path to wholeness will be centered on the one relationship that promises to free us from the constraints we put on ourselves through overeating or yo-yo dieting or self-loathing, from the things that prevent us from experiencing the peace and potential that is rightfully ours.

Jesus said: "I am the bread of life; whoever comes to me will never hunger, and whoever believes in me will never thirst" (John 6:35).

What are the things you are hungry for? Physical beauty? Acceptance? An escape from the chaos? A better job? A happier home life? Chances are good that whatever your hunger, you attempt to fill it with things that can't possibly give you what you're seeking.

Together we're going to travel a path that will lead us closer and closer to the truth—to our personal truth, to ultimate Truth. And once we've tasted that reality, that peace that only Jesus can give, only then will we know in our hearts the fulfillment of what Jesus offers us in the Gospel. Imagine for a moment breaking free from the constant craving, not just for the cookies you don't need but for a life different from the one you're living right now, for a you different from the one you're called to be. It's possible. You've already taken the first step.

So how should you use this book? You can work your way through it from beginning to end, or you can pick it up and find a chapter that speaks to you right now. You can read it on your own or find a buddy or even a group of friends to make this journey with you. Whatever approach you decide to take, I hope you'll see it as the beginning of a permanent change, a pivotal moment when you choose to become your true self and to know once and for all the meaning of God's all-embracing unconditional love, a love that requires no specific body mass index or dress size.

At the end of each chapter are meditations and questions for discussion or journaling. When you've finished the book, you can use the practical exercises in the appendix at the back to help you go forward. It's probably a good idea to have a notebook nearby as you read this book so you can jot down thoughts, memories, tips, and plans.

Before we set off on this journey, I'd like to share a story. When I was deciding whether I was really ready to sign on and do this book, I spent a lot of time praying on it. I wanted to be sure that it was the right thing, not only professionally but personally and spiritually as well. I really put it before God and asked for some insights. Then I went to Sunday Mass, and, I kid you not, every single reading that day was focused on food.

The first reading began with this verse from Isaiah 25:6: "On this mountain the Lord of hosts will provide for all peoples a feast of rich food and choice wines, juicy, rich food and pure, choice wines." The second reading continued the theme with this gem from the Letter of St. Paul to the Philippians 4:12–13: "I have learned the secret of being well fed and of going hungry, of living in abundance and of being in need. I can do all things in him who strengthens me." And finally, in a reading from the Gospel of St. Matthew, Jesus compared the kingdom of heaven to a lavish wedding banquet.

I'm sure the priest that day wondered why I was sitting in the front row with a goofy smile on my face. It's rare that I get those without-a-doubt answers to prayers, but, boy, this one was right up there. More than that, however, those readings were a reminder—in black and white—that food and faith are inseparable. So, turn the page, come to the feast, and know what it means to never be hungry!

Chapter 1
A Deeper Hunger
Filling the spiritual void with food

You formed my inmost being;
You knit me in my mother's womb.
I praise you, so wonderfully you made me;
wonderful are your works.
Psalm 139:14

When was the first time you looked in the mirror and didn't like who you saw staring back at you? Were you still in elementary school, fighting back tears from the constant teasing over your weight, your eyeglasses, or your hair? Was it high school perhaps, when the prospect of getting a date for the prom shifted the feelings of inadequacy into high gear? Maybe you're one of the lucky ones who managed to make it into adulthood before you began to cringe every time you caught a glimpse of your reflection in the bathroom medicine cabinet.

Now for what is likely the more difficult question: When was the *last* time you looked in the mirror and didn't like who you saw staring back at you? Twenty years ago? Two years ago? One week ago? Today?

I can remember walking into the confessional in our little parish chapel when I was no more than ten years old, kneeling down, and including among my list of very innocent sins: "I hate myself."

Despite my up-close-and-personal relationship with that feeling, I'm still dumbfounded by the fact that a child or teenager, or adult for that matter, can look in the mirror day after day and see only the flaws. And yet that feeling comes so naturally for some of us.

For far too many of us, learned feelings of inadequacy have led us to where we are today, fighting a daily battle to love ourselves for exactly who we are—for who God made us to be—and, more often than not, losing that battle to the very things that only take us deeper and deeper into our feelings of self-loathing. We attempt to feed our hunger—for God, for others, for love, for understanding, for success and more—with momentary bites that never satisfy.

On some level we imagine we can fill up all the empty places in our soul with other things, often fattening things—French fries and burgers, ice cream and cookies, bowls of pasta and bottles of wine. But after we wipe our mouths and throw away the evidence, all we have left are deep feelings of regret, guilt, sadness, and anger.

One morning not that long ago, when I was battling a boatload of disappointment and doubt in my own life, I found myself stealing jellybeans from my kids' candy collections. As I paced around my house, trying to ward off a downward spiral, I'd make periodic passes by their individual boxes of jellybeans sitting on our dining room sideboard. Although I was only semi-conscious of what I was doing at the time, I had the wherewithal to take some from each box so that no child's candy would be noticeably lower than the others'. It was only a few hours later, as I was getting ready to go out, that I realized the seemingly desperate hunger for food—candy, in this case—was really about a desperate need for something else, something that was missing in my life.

Every time I contemplated a particularly difficult work situation, I grabbed a handful of candy. When I thought about ways I felt

I was failing as a mother, I grabbed another fistful of candy. When I reflected on my spiritual life and stalled attempts at real prayer, you guessed it, I grabbed yet more candy. Not because I was hungry. Not because the candy was particularly good. But because there was a void in my life begging to be filled, and food is my go-to, all-purpose filler.

Even as I popped the jellybeans in my mouth, as if they were a magical cure for my emotional hangover, I knew I'd be sorry in the morning when my waistband felt tighter and the scale inched upward. And still I felt powerless to simply stop eating.

That scenario, unfortunately, is not an isolated instance in my life, or in the lives of so many other people, particularly women. From my earliest teenage days, I can remember starvation diets and candy bar binges during times of celebration or strife. If a pool party or school dance was coming, I'd exist on cans of Tab and sugarless gum. Literally. But more often than not I'd head to McDonald's with my super skinny best friend for French fries and shakes, or I'd walk over to the pizza parlor across the street from the card store where I worked part time to grab two slices and an orange soda, sometimes with a couple of pink snowball cupcakes on the side.

Although I've never been seriously overweight, I have still battled the dual demons of mindless eating and high-calorie habits on a regular basis. The older I get and the further along my spiritual path I walk, the more I have come to see these bad habits for what they are—ways to avoid what I really need, what I really want, what I crave and fear all at once.

Sometimes a Cookie Is Just a Cookie

Of course, not every bite of extra food we put into our mouths is a statement on our emotional or spiritual well-being. Sometimes we eat out of boredom or stress or without even realizing we are scarfing down handfuls of Goldfish crackers as we simultaneously help the kids with homework, cook dinner, and check email. We live in a society that pushes us to go faster and faster, to multitask our multitasking. Food just gets caught up in the mix.

I realized that fact in a big way after making my first silent retreat at the Pyramid Life Center in New York's Adirondack Mountains. This retreat was a little more intense than your typical silent retreat because we weren't allowed to read, write, or make casual contact. When you are sitting in a dining room with twenty other silent people, some just a few feet across from you, and you cannot distract yourself with a book or an iPod or a crossword puzzle, you suddenly come face-to-face with your plate of food, sometimes for the very first time. And it can be a little unsettling.

There is no place left to hide, when you are silently staring into a bowl of corn chowder with no access to all of the usual emotional crutches. And that's a good thing when we're talking about coming to terms with bad eating habits and unhealthy attitudes. Peering into my bowl that weekend, I began to see that the way to God is paved, at least in part, with more mindful eating, more mindful talking, more mindful living. Unfortunately, that lovely idea didn't last long after I returned to the real world and the insanity of home life, where even Grace Before Meals is fit for a circus tent.

The first "regular" day after my retreat, I sent the kids off to school and made myself breakfast. As I set it on the table, I began looking for a newspaper or magazine or laptop or phone. No sense wasting valuable eating time not getting something else done, right? And then I stopped. And listened. Quiet. Something that is so rare at our house. I could hear the tap-tapping of rain on the fallen leaves. I could hear the cats batting a toy around the basement. I could hear myself think. And I wondered, what exactly am I trying to drown out when

I insist on multitasking even while eating a meal in peace? It's one thing if the kids are home and I've got my mommy hat on. But when I have time to eat breakfast alone, why would I want to clutter it up with meaningless stuff? Because eating mindlessly is one of the ways I avoid thinking, one of the ways I avoid listening to God, one of the ways I get out of living in the moment. I'm much better at living in the next moment or the next year.

So that morning I put away the newspapers. In fact, I removed them from sight. I cleared the space around my seat of any clutter. I put the phone in the other room. I even lit a prayer candle in the center of the table. And I sat down, said a blessing, and slowly and quietly ate my oatmeal with walnuts and dried cranberries, tasting every bite. I found, as I did on my silent retreat, that eating in silence is a lot like praying in silence. I had to keep bringing myself back to that spoon of food every time my mind wanted to craft an email in my head or think about what was up next on our family calendar.

When you slowly and prayerfully taste every bite of your food, you do not overeat, and you don't go looking for something else five minutes later. It clears a space inside and allows God to enter into the picture, which, I can tell you from experience, is a powerful way to shift eating from mindless to mindful, something we'll discuss in very practical terms in chapter 7. Obviously silent meals are not the norm and they never will be for those of us living out in the world, but there are important lessons to be learned there, and we'll explore them as we journey toward wholeness.

Are You Willing to Be Radical?

Best-selling author Anne Lamott, in her book *Traveling Mercies: Some Thoughts on Faith*, writes about her battle with both bulimia and alcoholism. She confesses her realization, after finally getting sober, that the binging and purging that controlled her life were never really about the food but about something much, much deeper.

"I felt when I got sober, God had saved me from drowning, but now I was going to get kicked to death on the beach. It's so much hipper to be a drunk than a bulimic," she writes, speaking of the internal "voice" that would haunt her until she went to the store and bought Cheetos and chocolates and laxatives.

Lamott goes on to explain how she eventually reached her limit and sought help, finally coming to terms with what it feels like to be truly hungry, as opposed to eating mindlessly when something inside—whether we call it a voice or a feeling or a habit—urges us to forage in the pantry or stare into the refrigerator or run to the store. She calls her ability to accept herself as she is and overcome her bulimia a "miracle."

"I know where I was, and I know where I am now, and you just can't get here from there. Something happened that I had despaired would never happen," she writes. "Whatever it was, learning to eat was about learning to live—and deciding to live; and it is one of the most radical things I've ever done."

There's no doubt that any major life change requires a radical shift in thinking. If we have always thought of ourselves as fat or ugly or invisible or all of the above, learning to see ourselves with new eyes can feel more dangerous than skydiving or swinging from a trapeze without a net. Even if we aren't facing anything close to the devastating and dangerous condition that Lamott battled, it's still not easy to change the negative tape that has been on continuous loop for years, maybe forever.

So it comes down to asking ourselves the questions we've probably been trying to avoid: What do we want from life? What are our hopes and fears? Where is God in the mix and how do we relate to our Creator in contemplation, in action, in the mundane details of daily life? Are we willing to be radical, willing to accept a miracle in our own lives?

As you work your way through this book, try to become more aware of your eating habits. I'm not talking about counting calories or carbs. I'm talking about a general, guilt-free awareness. Don't attach judgment to anything. Just observe. If you find yourself eating chips straight from the bag as you talk on the phone, make a mental (or actual) note of who you're talking to and what you're talking about. If you're sitting at your desk popping chocolate chip cookies like they're peanuts, make a note of what you're working on or what might have transpired in the minutes before or what is coming up on your agenda that day. If you're sitting home alone on a Friday night with a gallon of ice cream and a spoon, think about what you'd rather be doing at that moment. Chances are there's something happening on a spiritual or emotional plane that's coming out in a physical way—in this case, through eating.

At the same time, reflect on where you are in your spiritual life. Is your relationship with God what you want it to be? If not, what's lacking and what can you do to bridge the gap? Start to look at your body and spirit as two parts of a whole. We cannot attempt to pursue one piece without impacting the other. Are we always rushing and seeking? Slow down and breathe. Before you reach for that next cookie, sandwich, chip—stop. Try to decipher whether you are really, truly, physically hungry or starving for something else. Pray. Talk to God. Lean on Jesus. Make a spiritual Communion, taking the nourishment you need from the Source of all fulfillment.

When we begin to connect prayer lives to physical lives, when we look beneath the surface, we often discover just how deeply intertwined the two are and how our food issues are wound around our spiritual needs and longings. We're not hungry for a carton of ice cream or a bag of chips. We're hungry for acceptance—from ourselves even more than from others—for love, for fulfillment, for peace. We're hungry for a life we think we don't deserve or can't have, for the person we know we can be if only we'd give ourselves the chance.

Often, it is not the fear of failure that holds us back but the fear of success. We cling to the comfortable rather than step out into the possible. So we sit at home with a container of Cookies and Cream rather than take a chance on getting our heart broken again, or we down an entire bag of chocolate-covered pretzels rather than work on that resume that might get us out of a dead-end job. Or we eat cold pasta right from the refrigerator rather than sit down in silence and listen for the whisper of the Spirit speaking to our hearts.

In her beautiful poem "The Summer Day," Mary Oliver asks the question that really lies at the heart of our battle to reclaim our lives from bad habits, escapes, and addictions: "What is it you plan to do with your one wild and precious life?"[1]

How would you answer that question right now, without over-thinking it? What do you want to do with your "one wild and precious life"? With each chapter of this book, we'll attempt to answer that question by peeling back layers to expose the core of our true selves, the beings so wonderfully made by our Creator God. In doing that, we make the radical decision to live fully, just as we are, and to learn to love what we see in the mirror, not in a vain or pretentious way, but in a healthy, holistic, and holy way.

You may be thinking that this plan sounds difficult, or next to impossible. For sure, it won't be easy, but the road we've been walking until now hasn't exactly been problem-free. So how do we start? By taking the time to pay attention to the world around us. By learning to be idle without needing to fill up the empty space with noise or busyness—or food. By digging down into our souls to discover our real reasons for filling up on cookies and potato chips and candy when we want to fill up on God and goodness and joy. By becoming more mindful of how we eat, where we eat, when we eat, and what we eat.

We'll talk about all of this in detail, step-by-step, as we journey through this book, so don't feel overwhelmed and don't feel as though you are doing this alone. Countless people, myself included, have been on this same path or are on it right now with you.

What Are You Hungry For?

A few years ago, when I was preparing for a presentation I was to make at a women's retreat, I spent time reflecting on Psalm 139, which is partially quoted at the start of this chapter. When I first read the psalm, I could feel walls going up. I bristled at the idea that I could be "wonderfully" made. I was reading and shaking my head, no, no, no. There's a good chance you may feel the same way when you soak in the full version of the psalm below.

Read it now, not as a psalm written thousands of years ago but as a poem written for you, *by* you, today. Quiet everything around you and rest in the words of this psalm. Let the beautiful images wash over you and carry you along, and if you feel the walls starting to go up, acknowledge the feelings and then let them go.

Lord, you have probed me, you know me:
 you know when I sit and stand;
 you understand my thoughts from afar.
My travels and my rest you mark;
 with all my ways you are familiar.
Even before a word is on my tongue,
 Lord, you know it all.
Behind and before you encircle me
 and rest your hand upon me.

Such knowledge is beyond me,
  far too lofty for me to reach.
Where can I hide from your spirit?
  From your presence, where can I flee?
If I ascend to the heavens, you are there;
  if I go down to the depths, you are there too.
If I fly with the wings of dawn
  and alight beyond the sea,
Even there your hand will guide me,
  your right hand holds me fast.
If I say, "Surely darkness shall hide me,
  and night shall be my light"—
Darkness is not dark for you,
  and night shines as the day.
  Darkness and light are but one.
You formed my inmost being;
  you knit me in my mother's womb.
I praise you, so wonderfully you made me;
  wonderful are your works!
My very self you knew;
  my bones were not hidden from you,
When I was being made in secret,
  fashioned as in the depths of the earth.
Your eyes foresaw my actions;
  in your book all are written down;
  my days were shaped, before one came to be.

Psalm 139:1–16

After I'd spent some serious time with that psalm and really started to believe it was something written for me, something that was not just meant to be read with my head but instead experienced with my heart, I felt a subtle shift inside. It was as if someone had gently nudged the skipping record of negative thoughts that had been so much a part of my internal conversation, enabling me to hear the next line of my life song. That's not to say all the negativity vanished in a flash, but a door opened up and a slant of light slipped in.

What if God really does love me unconditionally? What if I really am wonderfully made? What if it's possible to turn around all those years of thinking I was "less than"? What if . . . what if . . . what if?

If we believe we are made by our Creator to be exactly who and what we are—nothing more, nothing less, nothing better, nothing worse—we can begin to let go of some of the shackles that bind us to false ideas of physical beauty and outward appearance. We can finally look inside and discover our true selves and the wellspring of love that is the Spirit of God within us. And when we connect with that Spirit, we can face the mirror and believe, really believe, that we are *more than* because we are loved by a God who wants to give us everything we can imagine and far more.

When we do that, or even take the first baby steps in that direction, we find, almost without realizing it, that our need for other things, whether food or alcohol, shopping or obsessive cleaning, suddenly begins to lessen. The good feelings we tried to obtain through an extra slice of pizza or a hot fudge sundae are now suddenly there for the taking. No spoon required. No calories to count. And the news gets even better. When we finally see ourselves for who we really are and not for who we imagine ourselves to be, or who society tells us we should be, we discover we can eat the foods we love and be healthy and happy all at the same time. It's not an all-or-nothing proposition; it never was.

Food for Thought

1. How did you feel when you read Psalm 139? What feelings came up? Can you see yourself as "wonderfully" made?

2. Have you seen yourself as "less than" at any point in your life? If so, what brings that feeling up for you?

3. Are you more inclined toward emotional eating or mindless eating?

4. Can you pinpoint triggers that send you looking for the nearest box of cookies or bag of chips? Is it work-related, relationship-related, spiritual, physical?

5. Are you willing to consider that you are perfect just as you are and begin to look at yourself and your life with new eyes?

6. Think of at least one friend who could share this journey with you, someone who will listen when you need to talk, encourage you when you're losing ground, celebrate and pray with you when you're making strides.

7. Get a notebook or journal and begin to record your reactions to what you're reading—your food habits, prayer habits, triggers, urges, anything that will help you uncover what's at the heart of your relationship with food.

Practice

Begin to look at yourself as a "wonderfully made" whole—body and soul, two critical pieces working in cooperation. Reflect on how you nourish your spirit compared to how you nourish your body. Do you overfeed one and starve the other? How can you add more spiritual food to your daily life to balance out the equation? Can you do more spiritual reading or silent prayer? Can you get to daily Mass on occasion or pray the Rosary or Divine Office?

Find one spiritual exercise that suits you and make a commitment to add it to your daily routine for one week. When you feel yourself getting overwhelmed by negative feelings or food cravings, turn back to your spiritual practice or to the words of Psalm 139 and try to settle into the calm, quiet space you find there.

At the week's end, notice if there were any changes in your eating habits and attitudes during this time of regular prayer. Were you more accepting of yourself and your weaknesses? Did you have more or fewer bouts of negativity or food binges? Write down what you found. Can you continue your practice long-term or adapt it to fit more easily into your life? Make a prayer plan.

Meditation

So often we look in the mirror
as if through a glass darkly,
seeing not what God has created
but what we have created
in our own minds, our own hearts.
We pray today for the grace
and the wisdom to look beyond
the surface, to see into
our own souls and recognize
the hand of God at work there.
We are wonderfully made,
known and loved by our Creator
before we ever drew breath.

Chapter 2
Dieting Delusion
Food is not the enemy

Our deepest fear is not that we are inadequate.

Our deepest fear is that we are powerful beyond measure.

It is our Light, not our darkness, that most frightens us.

*We ask ourselves, who am I to be brilliant,
gorgeous, talented, and fabulous?*

Actually, who are you not to be? You are a child of God.

Marianne Williamson

Louise was only fifteen years old when her neighbor went on a diet and inspired her to do the same. Already used to being told she was "cute and chubby" by a long list of relatives, Louise's skewed view of her body and her self-worth was well on its way to becoming her default perspective. That first teenage diet didn't work; in fact, it made her sick. But it started her on a lifelong journey of dieting as a way to reach self-acceptance.

"I continued to diet. I tried everything—Weight Watchers, Atkins, low-fat, you name it," says Louise, who acknowledges that stress is her "trigger" point. "I have to be very careful when I'm stressed not to shove food in abundance into my mouth. I try to keep food in its place, but afterward I find I'm eating for absolutely no reason. The more I eat, the more disgusted I feel, so the more I eat."

Sound familiar? I know it did to me. Louise's answers to my questions could have been my own, word for word. In the spirit of full disclosure, Louise is my aunt, and, for the record, she is simply stunning at sixty-something years old—a perfect reminder that this obsession with dieting and appearance often has nothing to do with how we really look or how much we weigh.

Much like Louise, I, too, started dieting around fifteen or sixteen, when years of hearing it was too bad I had inherited "athletic" legs—which was a code word for "fat"—left me thinking I needed to change my appearance to be considered pretty or thin or both. I remember one diet where I ate nothing but bananas one day, nothing but grapefruit the next, and nothing but vegetables another. Over the years, I tried diets of meal replacement drinks, variations on Weight Watchers, and even outright near-starvation for a few months, something I'll talk about in more detail a little later.

Mind you, other than when I was losing "baby weight" after my pregnancies, I've never had to lose more than ten pounds, fifteen at the most. But I clung to those diets and to the belief that those few pounds would make the difference between being an unhappy, unlovable human being and being a confident, happy person. I'm obviously not alone in that conviction.

"Why five pounds would change my looks, feelings, confidence, and happiness is beyond me, but I'm constantly striving for that, and, when I get there and love the feeling, I sabotage it," says Louise, who is a wife, mother, grandmother, avid runner, and director of administration at her office. "I don't know how to break out of the vicious cycle except stay the way I am—five pounds heavier—and love it."

It's amazing what we can do to ourselves, isn't it? We can hang our self-worth on five or ten pounds, or a pant size, or a false image we see in a magazine or on TV. But I think Louise hit the nail on the head when she spelled out how and why food and self-worth are so connected in her own life:

> Dieting and food are definitely connected to how I feel about myself and my life. If I can control my eating, I feel good; I think I look good. That's probably the key. If I'm in control of my eating, I'm in control of my life, and then I can accomplish whatever I want because I feel no one can beat me down.

Control—that ever-elusive dream. We all crave it, and yet our faith reminds us that we're never really in control. We may try to convince ourselves otherwise, but usually we find out the hard way that even our best attempts to steer every last detail of our lives won't give us what we're seeking. So part of our effort to break free of the dieting delusion, the mistaken belief that we can manipulate our future—or our present—by how much or how little we eat, is learning to let go of those false images, misguided dreams, and impossible goals, and to put ourselves in God's hands. Knowing what we need to do, however, doesn't make it easy. We still manage to mire ourselves in self-doubt and harsh judgment.

I've been on the darker side of this battle, and it wasn't pretty. I was just finishing up my freshman year of college, heading into summer, when I decided I wanted to lose a few pounds. I started tracking every calorie I ate, charting my measurements by the day, sometimes by the hour, writing everything in a notebook, and exercising like mad to offset what I was taking in. What started as a casual diet quickly spiraled into something verging on the beginnings of an eating disorder. I remember how worried my mother was when she saw the pounds dropping away as I found creative ways to get out of eating dinner.

I existed on saltine crackers and cucumber salads made with a vinegar and Sweet-n-Low "dressing." Five, ten, fifteen pounds fell off in less than a month. If I ate even a salad for dinner, I would go upstairs and exercise to the point of total exhaustion. Dinner at a relative's house? I packed my saltines. Forced (by mom) to eat dinner on the deck with the family? I managed to spill my drink, ruin my dinner and my clothes, and leave the table.

And then came the tipping point. My family was headed to Wildwood Crest, New Jersey, for our annual vacation, and I was expected to join them. If you've spent any time on the Jersey Shore, you know that nothing—and I mean nothing—is low-calorie. They fry everything, even the Oreos. So there, wearing my new bathing suit with my bones sticking out at odd angles, I was forced to make a decision: eat nothing at all or eat something fattening. Eventually I gave in and ate a piece of pizza, and that one single event broke the cycle for me. By week's end I think I even ate a *zeppoli*, which is deep-fried dough. I had been saved. I didn't regain all the weight, but I did reach a happy medium eventually. I was lucky to break free so quickly and so easily. But even after that dangerous diet attempt had passed, the core issue remained: I still believed my worth could be measured in pounds.

Back in those days, I was frantically trying to get all As in college while I worked for an accounting firm during my "off" hours, answered phones at our local parish on the weekend, and sang in a band at night. I was burning the candle at both ends, feeling totally out of control, and food became the one thing I could have absolute say over. Although I didn't see it when I was in the midst of it, in hindsight it is as obvious as a neon billboard.

Even today, the control myth can take hold of me. I can feel totally confident and positive about myself and my life if my clothes fit a little loose and the scale shows me the right number. A few pounds in the wrong direction and my mood, my day, my life can take on an aura of unhappiness and dissatisfaction, not only with my looks but with just about everything. And that's the crux of what we're dealing with here. Whether we have to lose a hundred pounds or ten pounds, our self-worth should not—cannot—hang on a number or a diet plan. It has to be rooted in something deeper, something true, if we can ever hope to put a stop to these endless efforts to mold ourselves into someone else's image of beauty or health or perfection. The first step toward that freedom is the acknowledgment, in the words of Alcoholics Anonymous, that only "a Power greater than ourselves could restore us to sanity."

For us, that "Power" is Jesus Christ, the only Way to true peace, acceptance, and balance. Of course, turning our lives and our wills over to God is easier said than done. If it were as simple as making a decision, our world would be a very different place. Saying and doing are two very different things. So we're going to need to dig down into places we might not readily want to go and confront feelings we may have never shared with another soul.

Getting Beyond Self-Sabotage

Life is hard enough. We really can't afford to be our own worst enemies. And yet, that's often the case. We battle unnecessary guilt over how we look and what we eat. We put in long months of exercising and eating right and the mental and emotional effort that goes into feeling good about ourselves. Then, when we finally feel great, we often do the one thing—or eat the one thing—that will set a destructive cycle in motion. Why? Often it's because we don't think we deserve to feel good. Other times it can be a physical response, even an addiction, that causes our backsliding.

We back away from feelings of happiness and self-satisfaction, as if feeling okay with our appearance, our work, our lives is a sign of vanity, or a jinx, or just plain impossible. We hear those voices from our childhoods, or maybe our present, the ones that tell us we are not good enough for one reason or another. And we respond, usually in negative ways, undoing our hard work and fulfilling all those false prophecies about being "chubby" or "athletic" or "stocky" or whatever term has been used to describe us.

In many ways, our Church hasn't helped matters, often being inconsistent in its approach to the human body and bodily pleasures. Yes, there are plenty of Scripture verses that remind us that we are temples of the Holy Spirit, that we are "wonderfully made," but there are just as many that remind us of the weaknesses and flaws of our humanness. Over the centuries, that's been compounded with additions from various sources, from a too-heavy focus on the asceticism of the Desert Fathers to the more modern but mistaken belief that self-acceptance and self-love are vain and sinful rather than healthy and inspired by God. As a result, many of us come to believe that hating our body is holier or spiritually superior to accepting our body as good or even beautiful.

But if you look beyond the surface-level Catholic guilt over anything good as it relates to the body, the reality is far different. The *Catechism of the Catholic Church* says, "Life and physical health are precious gifts entrusted to us by God" (2288), and it goes on to explain that we are required to respect our bodies while avoiding what it calls the "cult of the body," which is an obsession with physical perfection and athletic prowess.[1]

"The virtue of temperance disposes us to avoid every kind of excess: the abuse of food, alcohol, tobacco, or medicine," the *Catechism* states (2290).

Even when we look at the harsh sacrifices of the Desert Fathers, there is room for a broader understanding, one that does not center on loathing the body but on feeding the soul. In the introduction to her book *The Desert Fathers: Sayings of the Early Christian Monks*, Benedicta Ward writes that the monks did not see food and wine as bad in and of themselves but as temptations that might distract them from their prayer.

"They did not talk, not because they hated conversation, but because they wanted to listen intently to the voice of God in silence; they did not dislike eating, but were feeding on the word of God so that they did not have room for earthly food or time to bother with it."[2]

In *Gaudium et Spes*, the *Pastoral Constitution on the Church in the Modern World*, which came out of the Second Vatican Council, we hear this take on the significance of humanity:

> Though made of body and soul, man is one. Through his bodily composition he gathers to himself the elements of the material world; thus they reach their crown through him, and through him raise their voice in free praise of the Creator. For this reason man is not allowed to despise his bodily life, rather he is obliged to regard his body as good and honorable since God has created it and will raise it up on the last day.[3]

Unfortunately most of us didn't get those positive Catholic messages on our physicality growing up. The Church's nuanced teachings on the body were lost behind the flashier "headlines" about sinfulness. And so, many Catholics grew up with the off-target belief that feeling bad about our bodies and ourselves in general made us better people, or at least better Catholics.

Self-hatred of that kind, however, is really narcissism on its head, an upside-down kind of egoism that focuses all our energy and thoughts on self in an attempt to prove how unworthy we are. It's really no different than the opposite extreme, the person who primps and preens in front of a mirror because she thinks she looks so good. Two sides of the same unbalanced coin. Neither is healthy; neither brings peace.

"The hardest thing for us is to assess ourselves. We are very black and white. That's a core issue—all or nothing, good or bad," says Merci Miglino, a life coach, public speaker, and author of *From Doormat to Diva: Taking Center Stage in Your Own Life*, who has had her own battles with weight loss and self-esteem. She suggests we take some lessons on what she calls "kind regard" directly from scripture.

In the Book of Isaiah we hear how loved we are: "Do not be afraid, I am with you" (41:10). "I have called you by name; you are mine" (43:1). "Upon the palms of my hands I have written your name" (49:16).

"That's kind regard," Merci says of the scripture readings. "Pray from that place, and, from the courage of that place, look for the inconvenient truth."

What *is* the inconvenient truth? Those things about ourselves that we don't like to admit—the blaming or complaining we do to shift the onus away from ourselves, the belief that five pounds will radically change our lives, the hurtful comments we've turned into ultimate truths, the fear that losing weight will make us invisible, or, conversely, too free or too powerful.

"We operate with these unconscious beliefs. They're always irrational, but they always have a teensy weensy bit of truth to them that we blow up to be the whole," says Merci. "We have to appreciate that there's physicality to this belief, like you have worn a path in your brain. If you've worn a path in your living room carpet, you always tend to walk in that same place. You don't even realize that you're doing this, but by doing it over and over you program yourself."

Merci speaks from experience. Her mother had a weight problem, which quickly became her own. Merci started taking diet pills at age ten and spent many years gaining and losing weight, believing that if she solved her weight problem, everything would be okay.

"I lost weight with much success and gained it back with the same success," she says, explaining that her beliefs about herself, some of which made little sense, were at the core of her yo-yo dieting. What kinds of beliefs? Things like this: If I'm fat, then I am safe from unwanted attention, or I'll be in control of my life, or I'll be more than a pretty face, or I won't need anyone so no one can disappoint me.

"It was the work of examining these beliefs that began a long journey to acceptance and self-love. When I began to take on new beliefs—such as, 'I am loved. I can be in control without overeating. I can be safe in the world. I can be light and significant at the same time'—I began to rely less and less on food as a source of comfort," says Merci. "It was very gradual, and it was coupled with a shift that had me moving more than I usually do, through yoga and walking and running."

Off the Beaten Path

Despite all those changes, however, the weight still didn't drop off for Merci, due to what she believes is a genetic predisposition to weight gain and a "battered metabolism" resulting from too much dieting, including years of on-and-off starvation. So a few years ago, she made a very "willful" decision. She had gastric bypass surgery.

"Despite many fits and starts, it has been a miracle," Merci says, adding that anyone who thinks surgery is the "easy way out" has no idea how far off base they are. "I thought about it for two years. I prayed about it," she recalls, saying that one life coach she consulted asked her who her "spirit guides" were. Merci quickly responded: the Blessed Mother. She prayed for Mary's help and went ahead with the gastric bypass. On the day of the surgery, a nurse named Mary was assigned to care for her. Then Merci returned home and realized her surgery had taken place on the Feast of Our Lady of Guadalupe. These were significant spiritual signs for her on the journey to physical wholeness, although she had never doubted the power of prayer.

"People will ask me how I did it. I can tell you some of it, but most of it was through prayer, asking and letting go," says Merci, explaining that "success" requires awareness, acceptance without judgment, and action. "I took drastic measures. Sometimes we need to take action and pray to step into that action. This life is work. It's the job of being saved or purified or unified."

Merci, who was once a hundred pounds overweight, says the "rigor of mindfulness" has kept her on track. As she spoke with me one morning in a local coffee shop, she nibbled on a scone the size of a dinner plate, eating only a tiny fraction of the bakery treat. Although I could have assessed her behavior just by watching her that day, Merci explained that "mindfulness" means she pays attention to what she eats, how she eats, and when she eats, but she also enjoys eating. You can't "demonize" food or "white knuckle it" every time you have to go to an office party or take your kids out for ice cream, she says.

So there has to be a balance, in our eating and in our lives. Yes, willpower is good, but we have to feel as if we're receiving something as well. I thought about that as Merci continued taking tiny bites of her scone while I sat with nothing but black coffee in front of me, in an effort to "be good." Some things never change, not unless we make a conscious effort to change them.

In his book *The End of Overeating: Taking Control of the Insatiable American Appetite*, David Kessler, MD, says that breaking these engrained food habits is not a question of simple mind-over-matter thinking. "Habits develop when familiar stimuli activate well-established neural pathways that produce repetitive behavior. . . . A substantial body of scientific research attests to this: Researchers have been able to measure movement before subjects know they're going to move. Brain activity stimulates a motor response in advance of awareness."[4]

He explains there's a difference between "goal-directed" behavior and "habit-directed" behavior. For example, in goal-directed eating, you might come home with a plan to make a bowl of pasta and then do just that. With habit-directed eating, you might walk into your house after work and go to the fridge without thinking because that's what you've done every day for the past ten years. Before you realize it, you're eating cold pizza while going through the mail. In the case of the habit-directed behavior, the repetition—like the worn path in the carpet Merci described earlier—affects our behavior before we have a chance to think it through. "Once the script becomes imprinted in the brain, the behavior it dictates becomes so routine that we can respond before we're even conscious of the stimuli," Kessler writes.[5]

The good news is that the same habit-response behavior that can cause us to eat food before we even realize what we're doing can be turned on itself to work in our favor. We just have to begin to lay the groundwork for new habits, which is what we'll try to do in the pages of this book.

If we want to reclaim our bodies and our lives, we need to adopt a multi-pronged approach to our food habits: choosing healthier foods, reshaping old habits, and refocusing our spiritual energy. By using the body-mind-soul approach, we come at our issues from every side, giving ourselves a much better chance of succeeding and grounding our plans in something deeper, something eternal.

Necessary Evils

Some people really do need diet plans—to lower cholesterol, to keep diabetes in check, to prevent heart disease or other conditions, to simply feel better and be less tired and more content. But too often the diets we choose are just plain awful and sometimes dangerous. They offer big promises in little pills and packets, trying to make us believe we can be transformed with little effort and in nearly no time at all. But true transformation comes from within.

If you are overweight and in need of a healthy eating plan, talk to your doctor. He or she can help you get a handle on what type of diet and exercise will work best for you and your health needs, but getting a list of "allowed" foods isn't enough to make comprehensive change. Once you've got a basic plan, it's time to get down to the really hard work: investigating your spiritual and emotional beliefs along with your physical habits. Those interior feelings are the things that may set you on a course for perpetual weight loss-gain and personal dissatisfaction. In fact, your interior feelings may be the very things that set those "habit-driven" behaviors into motion in the first place. If you don't get at the interior stuff, the exteriors will be next to impossible to carry out.

"If you need that buffer that food provides and your beliefs (about yourself) are profound, you will gain the weight back. Real change requires a shift in consciousness," says Merci. You can use any weight-loss method you want, she adds, but if you don't look at your underlying attitudes about yourself and put food in its appropriate place in your life, you will slip back into old bad habits no matter how much you've lost or how hard you've worked.

That's because so much of this dieting delusion is wrapped up in low self-esteem. We think we're not worthy. We imagine we need to do something in order to be lovable. We attempt to find that "something" through diet, but because our issues go far deeper than what we see in the mirror or on the scale, we are easily thrown into a tailspin when dieting doesn't change who we are at our core. It comes down to seeing ourselves as more than the sum of separate parts or pounds.

"It's about reunifying who we really are," says Merci. "You need to release this belief that you are not worthy. You are no better than anyone else; you are no worse than anyone else. Under every single issue, including weight, are pride—I am not good enough—and its sister, shame."

To reach that peaceful place of acceptance and balance takes a commitment of strength, time, and energy, something that Merci experienced firsthand. It also takes a willingness to seek outside help—both earthly and divine.

"I worked on it spiritually, emotionally, and physically. I worked to stop the pattern of harshly judging myself, to hold myself in kind regard," she recalls. "This isn't indulgent or condoning; it is a great place to find the Divine within, which calms all things. Prayer, mindfulness, mediation are essential for me."

Actually, those three things—prayer, mindfulness, and meditation—are essential for all of us as we walk this path. Deep inquiry requires deep prayer. Again we see that these seemingly opposite things—body and spirit, food and faith, diet and prayer—are powerfully connected. We cannot come to know our true selves without prayer, without that connection to our Creator, and we cannot find that place of balance without knowing our true selves.

In his book *Becoming Who You Are*, Jesuit Father James Martin writes about his own experience uncovering his true self:

> Early in the novitiate, I thought that being holy meant changing an essential part of who I was, *suppressing* my personality, not building on it. I was eradicating my natural desires and inclinations, rather than asking God to sanctify and even perfect them. Here's the way I thought about it: I knew that I certainly wasn't a holy person, so therefore being holy must mean being a different person. As strange as it sounds, I thought that being myself meant being someone else.[6]

How many of us feel that same way? So often when we latch onto a diet we do it out of the belief that if we can become someone else, someone thinner, someone "prettier" by society's standards, we will finally be the person we were meant to be. But what if we take an entirely different tack, a radical tack? What if you are exactly who you are meant to be, and will become an even more perfect version of yourself if only you are willing to drop the mask, step out of your own shadow, and embrace your true, wonderful, beautiful-as-is self?

So often we imagine that we would have value if only we could stop the stresses in our lives, if only we could fit into our twenty-year-old jeans, if only we could weigh 120 pounds. The list goes on and on. No matter what illusory "us" we envision, it comes down to a question of self-worth. What does it mean to be valued? Is our image based in reality or mirage? In many cases, we may say we want to be valued and recognized for who we are, and yet the thought of allowing our real selves to shine through is often the very thing that sends us running back to the bag of potato chips.

We are, as the Marianne Williamson quotation at the start of this chapter says, more afraid of our light than our darkness. We often choose to hide in the dark of extra pounds, baggy clothes, and overly restrictive diets because weight lets us be invisible, and sometimes we think it's easier to go through life being invisible. What would it mean to be visible, not just for who you are on the outside, but for who you are as a total package? Imagine the possibilities.

If God has called you by name, if your name is engraved upon God's palm, how can you be unacceptable or inferior in any way? What is it you believe that keeps you from embracing your true self and God's love for you just as you are? Is it really a diet that you need to "fix" you, or perhaps some serious one-on-one time between God and your true self?

Looking back at the stories in this chapter, we see clearly that the diet delusion can be forced to fit our needs, whatever they may be. Louise's story and my own demonstrate the ways we try to control our lives and create an aura of strength by depriving ourselves of food. On the flip side of that same mentality is Merci, who used the opposite approach in an attempt to achieve the same goal. For her, overeating became her method of choice. Starvation and gluttony are opposite on the surface but closely connected when we dig deeper. Both are misguided paths to self-acceptance and self-worth. Both pull us away from the truth and mire us on a road to nowhere. There is only one true path, and that has to begin with God and expand both outward and inward through prayer and mindfulness, non-judgment and self-love.

Of course, moving ourselves off that well-worn path takes hard work. It's far easier to battle fifty pounds of excess weight in the light of day than wrestle with destructive personal demons in the silence of our hearts. We desperately cling to the idea that the perfect fad diet will give us our heart's desire, that a packet of dehydrated food will magically turn us into the person God created us to be. But there are no quick fixes here. Dieting doesn't work that way. *Life* doesn't work that way.

At this point, most of us have tried everything but the one thing that can truly change us: God. When we shift our focus away from our false perceptions and onto the love poured out for us in the person of Jesus Christ, we begin to take those first steps away from the path of self-hatred and self-destruction, out of the darkness and into the light of life.

Food for Thought

1. Our first order of business is to become *aware* of our beliefs. What do you believe about yourself? What comments, voices, images haunt your private thoughts?

2. Can you acknowledge that those beliefs are false or exaggerated or irrational? How do those beliefs trigger food-related habits? Write down the connections.

3. Next on our "to do" list is acceptance. How can you shift from judgment to "kind regard" for yourself?

4. How do you feel when you think about God holding you in his palm, or calling you by name? Does it change your view of yourself? If so, how?

5. Finally, we need to take *action*. What are some alternatives to eating, things you can choose to do when those negative feelings get stirred up? Write down some options and turn to them the next time you want to turn to the fridge.

6. If you need to diet for health reasons, seek medical advice. If, however, dieting is simply part of your quest to become someone else, to be a different you, spend some quiet time reflecting on

why you feel that need to change. Who wants you to change? What's the worst thing that could happen if you just choose to love yourself as you are?

7.   When you imagine yourself becoming the person you want to be, what scares you most? How do you feel about unleashing your true self? What would it be like to value yourself with no conditions attached?

Practice

For the next week keep a detailed food/prayer journal. Don't count calories or grams of fat. Don't measure everything you eat (unless you are required to do so for health reasons). This isn't about obsession or buying right back into the diet mentality. This is an exercise in awareness. Write down the full meals and the snacks, even the broken half cookie at the end of the bag. If you tend to skip meals even when you're hungry, note that as well.

Write down if and when you manage to fit prayer into your day and what kinds of spiritual practices you include. Note how you're feeling physically, emotionally, spiritually, and whether you've done any physical exercise, from taking an aerobics class or going for a nightly walk to using the stairs instead of the elevator at work.

At the end of the week, look back and see if you can spot any connections between stress, boredom, or other issues and mindless eating. Begin to look for ways to replace bad habits with healthy habits day by day. If you always eat a mid-morning snack even when you're not hungry, maybe you can replace it with a few minutes of quiet meditation. If you tend to look for dessert when you're eating lunch in the cafeteria with friends, consider taking a walk around the block as soon as you're done with your main meal. Big changes start small.

Meditation

We are so willing to believe
the negative voices that echo
in our hearts and heads,
the labels that make us think
we can never be good enough,
the words that cut like glass.
But our God has called us by name.
Our God holds us, treasures us,
loves us without conditions.
Is that enough for us?

Chapter 3
Mirror, Mirror
Discovering our true selves

*Love yourself—accept yourself—forgive yourself—
and be good to yourself, because without you
the rest of us are without a source of many wonderful things.*
Leo F. Buscaglia

Every time I stand in line at the grocery store, I can't help but feel somewhat inadequate as I scan the unavoidable displays of women's magazines featuring impossibly beautiful people with perfect proportions, perfect skin, perfect hair, and perfect clothes. I know all about the tricks that are used to make even the most gorgeous models look better than they do in real life, modern-day versions of air brushing, and yet I can't help but buy into those images—if only subconsciously—and judge myself according to society's definition of beauty.

Even as I warn my daughters about what they see—wishing I could shield them from the onslaught of body-image fallacies that come at them from every corner of our culture—I continue to hold myself to the twisted standards I rail against. I tell my tween daughter that she's perfect just as she is, but I can't find a way to believe it about myself. We have been sold a bill of goods about body image, and most of us have signed on the dotted line, sacrificing our self-worth for someone else's vision of what and who we should be.

At home, in front of the mirror as we get dressed, we see the extra cookie we ate after everyone was asleep, the stretch marks from the last baby, the same ten pounds we lose and gain every few months or years, and we berate ourselves for not measuring up. We don't see our whole selves, the selves God made us to be. We see separate pieces, flaws, the things we don't like, and the sight can make us starve ourselves, or gorge ourselves, or just wallow in a perpetual state of self-disgust regardless of our diet, weight, size, or overall health.

Every once in a while, when I'm in plank position in yoga class or kicking into overdrive as I finish a morning run or hiking a nature trail with my kids, I experience the all-too-fleeting realization that I am blessed to have a body that is strong, healthy, and able to do things in middle age that many people can't do when they're young. I look around the exercise studio at the YMCA and see people of all ages, shapes, and sizes bending and stretching, running and climbing, and I am awed by our bodies' abilities to exceed our expectations. We truly are wonderfully made by God, and yet we rarely realize or acknowledge that truth.

So how can we learn to appreciate our bodies for the glorious creations they are, no matter what the circumstance? It comes down to reprogramming ourselves, in a sense. We have to find a way to erase the negative tape that's on continuous loop in our heads and replace it with something more positive, more realistic, more truthful. If we don't change the mantra of self-loathing, our feelings of inadequacy will continue to lead us deeper into bad diet plans, dangerous eating disorders, and a warped perspective that colors not just our eating habits but every aspect of our lives.

Take the Challenge

Here's an easy assignment, one that could end up being an eye-opening experience. If you, like me, have had body image issues throughout your life, you probably have an old photo or maybe multiple photos of yourself that demonstrate—if nowhere but in your own imagination—why you needed to lose weight. Go find that photo. Chances are you will look at it and wonder how you misjudged yourself, and so harshly. Where are the fat legs, the big hips, the thick waist?

I remember finding a photo of myself in my twirling uniform from my days as captain of the junior varsity squad at my high school. As I looked at myself in the dated, bright blue uniform and saddle shoes, I suddenly felt a sense of outrage. Wait a minute. I thought I had fat legs, "athletic legs." My legs were perfectly fine, normal, maybe even verging on thin. How and why was I so convinced that I was hideous, that I shouldn't wear shorts or a bathing suit, or, if I did, I should try to do my best to fade into the background and disappear off everyone's radar screen?

Find your photo and get outraged. Realize you were perfect then, just as you are perfect now, even if you need to lose some weight for health reasons. Stop looking at photos of yourself and seeing everything you think is wrong, because chances are, ten or fifteen years from now you can do this same exercise and realize that what you think of yourself today is just as off-base as those misjudgments and false ideas of your teenage or childhood years. The truth is, until you come to accept the person staring back at you from that photo, you'll never find a "happy" weight or size.

I see the beginnings of that kind of dissatisfaction in my own children, no matter how often I tell them how beautiful or handsome they are. My tween daughter, Olivia, will put on a winter ski parka and declare that it makes her "look fat." As I told her recently, she could put on a fat suit and still not look fat. She weighs sixty-five pounds soaking wet at age eleven. And yet she is already buying into that cultural definition of beauty as measured by the pound, or lack of pounds. Unfortunately, that attitude is not something we tend to outgrow.

"I remember having an epiphany while I watched a movie in my home one night. It was when I was still single and I was home by myself. In the movie, there is a character who has so many self-image and esteem issues and then one day she encounters the beauty of who she is in all of her body parts. At that moment—and not before and not really since—I felt an overwhelming awareness of how my body was of God and was beautiful no matter what," says Fran Rossi Szpylczyn, a Catholic blogger who has battled weight issues her entire life.

Fran says she was brought up with the "dual message" of eat/don't eat. Growing up in a New York Italian neighborhood, she learned to eat when she was happy, when she was sad, when she was hungry, and when she was not. Over the years, she has tried a variety of diet plans in an attempt to keep her weight in check.

"This is all absolutely about much more than food and diet. It is very much about a sense of being and of God. It is intimate, vulnerable and much greater than what is on the surface," she said. "Thinking about fads and so forth, I am reminded of how many people veer off from their Catholic faith and try other things. It is not necessarily all bad; it might just be what allows God to lead you right back to Christ. I think fad dieting is related to that, on a food level."

Words to Live By

Imagine what we could accomplish if we were to take all the energy we put into trying different diet plans and tearing ourselves down and use it for something more positive, something that will build us back up. If I were coming at this topic from a New Age perspective, this is where I'd give you lots of affirmations about self-love. But we don't need to fall back on empty affirmations that often make us feel more uncomfortable than more worthy. All we need to do is turn back to scripture, where we can hear again and again how much we are loved by our God. Is there any better affirmation than that?

Here's one of my favorite scripture passages, where Jesus reminds us that all our worrying about the surface stuff simply isn't worth our time and energy:

> Therefore I tell you, do not worry about your life, what you will eat or drink, or about your body, what you will wear. Is not life more than food and the body more than clothing? Look at the birds of the sky; they do not sow or reap, they gather nothing into barns, and yet your heavenly Father feeds them. Are not you more important than they? Can any of you by worrying add a single moment to your life-span? . . . Do not worry about tomorrow; tomorrow will take care of itself. (Mt 6:25–34)

Think for a moment about what your life would be like if you didn't worry about how you looked or what you were going to eat, or not eat. Kind of freeing, isn't it? Without all that worry, you just might have the energy to turn your attention toward something that could feed your soul in ways real food can't. Maybe you've always wanted to take a dance class. Maybe you'd like to try your hand at painting or pottery. Maybe you want to write a book or join a softball team. Maybe you want nothing more than to slow down and sit in silence. By letting go of the constant worry about our worthiness, we shine a light on those positive places that have been hiding in the shadows for too long. By bringing God into that space, we open up a whole new universe of possibility.

For too long we've lived with the notion that the only way to keep our weight in check, the only way to be good enough, is to worry about it constantly. We track every calorie, even if only in our minds, mentally adding up the pounds as we go. We keep clothes that are too big, or too small. We fear the holidays and the feasts that come with them, worrying our way through a family meal rather than savoring our time with loved ones. Does all that worry result in weight loss? Not usually. And when it does, it is typically fleeting.

When in Rome . . .

I took my first trip to Rome a couple of years ago, and I was prepared to come home about ten pounds heavier. I figured I'd easily pack on one pound for every day in the Eternal City, with its endless offerings of pastas and pastries and more. But I decided I wouldn't worry about weight because I wanted to enjoy this trip to the fullest. For eleven days, I seemed to be eating around the clock, starting with a daily power breakfast of cappuccino and *cornetti*, tender crescent-shaped dough confections. That was followed by platters of antipasto and steaming bowls of pasta for lunch and dinner, with carafes of local wine to wash it down and double scoops of gelato to top it off.

I returned home and gingerly stepped on the scale the next morning, as if sneaking up on it might give me a better reading. Voila! I had lost four pounds during my Roman eat-a-thon. How was it possible, I wondered? And more importantly, how could I replicate that recipe at home? When I reflected back, I realized that while I was eating big meals every day, I wasn't munching in between. There was no pantry or refrigerator luring me to the kitchen, where I could pick, pick, pick throughout the day. I ate a meal and then walked to my next destination. Walking was, of course, also part of the equation. I clocked miles every day as I made my way from St. Peter's Square to Santa Croce University through the Piazza Navona to my hotel and back again.

In Italy, food is an art form. You don't just run into McDonald's and grab a burger and fries that have been sitting under a heat lamp. You sit down, you eat slowly, you celebrate every bite. You don't fill up on tasteless snack foods throughout the day but instead gather with friends or family to feast on delicious food and interesting conversation. Worry? No worry. This is after all the land that gave us the term *la dolce vita*, the sweet life.

In a scene from the movie *Eat, Pray, Love*, based on the book by the same name, the Elizabeth Gilbert character and her friend Sofie go to Naples to get what is known as the best pizza in Italy. At first, Sofie just stares at her plate, unable to take a bite. She finally admits that she doesn't want to eat because she's getting a "muffin top."

"It is your moral imperative to eat and enjoy that pizza. . . . I am so tired of saying no and then waking up the next morning and recalling every single thing I ate the day before, every calorie I consumed so I know exactly how much self-loathing to take into the shower," says Elizabeth (played by Julia Roberts). "I am going for it. I have no interest in being obese; I am just through with the guilt."

Unfortunately many of us never allow ourselves the pleasure of just enjoying our food, of "going for it" with joyful abandon, because we are so wracked with guilt and self-hatred. We eat a delicious meal and feel bad, get on the scale and feel bad, in an endless cycle. We stare at our plates like Sofie and fear food, giving pizza or cake or potato chips the power to ruin our meal, our day, and our lives. And all the worry doesn't earn us a smaller waistband and a better self-image. In fact, it typically gets us just the opposite.

If I came away from my Roman experience with any "aha!" food insights, it was this: When we let go of the guilt and allow ourselves to enjoy our food, really enjoy every aspect of it—the sight of it, the smell of it, the taste of it, the feel of it, the people sharing it with us— we no longer feel deprived and we no longer feel as if we're "cheating." And when we let go of those negative emotions that are too often attached to eating, food tends to fall naturally into a more appropriate place.

"Even though we count calories, watch our weight, and figure fat grams, Americans are the fattest people in the world," writes Deborah Kesten, author of *Feeding the Body, Nourishing the Soul*. "What we've forgotten is that food is more than an amalgam of nutrients. Along with healing us physically, it enhances emotions, satisfies the soul, and connects us to others and to the mystery of life."[1]

Keston recommends getting back to what she calls an "enlightened diet," one that focuses not only on eating whole, fresh foods but on being grateful, uniting our eating with prayer, being aware of what we're eating and how we're eating, and sharing our meals with others, all things that we'll discuss in later chapters. But what she's saying is no different from what the Italians do every day, or what monastics do every day. Many cultures and most world religions have long recognized the significance of food for much more than simply physical nourishment and enjoyment.

In his bestselling book *Grace Before Meals*, Father Leo E. Patalinghug writes that sharing food has been "a way to strengthen relationships" since ancient cultures offered food to their gods.[2]

"In the Jewish Scriptures, we read how God sealed the covenant with his people through a meal. The relationship of food and faith is brought to a whole new level when Jesus becomes our Bread and Wine, a sign of the eternal covenant, with his family on earth! As a priest, you can imagine I take my theology very seriously," Fr. Patal-inghug writes. "Unfortunately, in today's fast-paced society, many of us have adopted a fast food mentality. We have forgotten that food is supposed to do more than just fill our stomachs."[3]

His book centers on the seemingly simple premise that grace before meals can transform our eating and our relationship with food, especially when shared around the family dinner table. Once again we see that when our focus moves away from guilt and self-image and calorie counting and toward a more holistic understanding of the role of food in our lives, diet becomes less complicated and more fulfilling. And slowly we begin to sever the ties that bind us to an eating mentality that is grounded in deprivation rather than celebration.

It's about balance. Learning to let go of the worry and guilt doesn't mean we let go of our goal of being a healthier weight or a healthier person. It means that we don't let our current size dictate our self-worth, and, in letting go of that constraint, we finally find ourselves free enough to become who we are meant to be in God's eyes.

Developing a New Attitude

Earlier we talked about taking out the "old tape," the one that plays on continuous loop in our heads, the one that says we're not good enough, we'll never be good enough unless we (fill in the blank) . . . lose five pounds, lose fifty pounds, drop a pants size, run a 5K. Now we're going to replace that with a new tape, one that will remind you on a daily basis that you are good enough as you are right this minute.

Tape a message to your bathroom mirror, or anywhere you'll see it early in the day and every day. If you'd like, include part of the earlier scripture quote: "Do not worry about tomorrow; tomorrow will take care of itself." Or maybe something from Psalm 139: "I praise you, God, so wonderfully you made me; wonderful are your works."

Or something even more simple. I once knew a priest whose motto was, "Smile, God loves you." How can you start the day unhappy when you've got those words staring you in the face? Find any scripture quote, prayer, or saying that inspires you to look past what you see in the mirror to the person God created you to be.

Again, this shouldn't be some empty platitude like the "Daily Affirmation with Stuart Smalley" skits by Al Franken on the old *Saturday Night Live* episodes. Franken perfectly captured the vapidness of such an approach with Stuart's catchphrase, "I'm good enough, I'm smart enough, and, doggonit, people like me." As Catholics, we recognize that true self-worth comes from something deeper, from receiving the unconditional love and mercy freely given to us by our Creator.

Hanging on my bathroom mirror is this prayer by St. Francis de Sales, which reminds me daily to let go of my worrying. I'm not always successful, but I'm always reminded.

Do not look forward in fear to the changes in life;
rather, look to them with full hope that as they arise,
God, whose very own you are,
will lead you safely through all things;
and when you cannot stand it,
God will carry you in his arms.
Do not fear what may happen tomorrow;
the same understanding Father who cares for
you today will take care of you then and every day.
He will either shield you from suffering
or will give you unfailing strength to bear it.
Be at peace,
and put aside all anxious thoughts and imaginations.

                                                                        St. Francis de Sales

You are God's very own. Do you believe that? Can you let that reality seep into your soul and take root? When we replace the negative tape with something centered in God, our worldview begins to change. Suddenly the pound or two we gained over Thanksgiving doesn't seem that scary or outrageous, the leftover birthday cake sitting on the counter doesn't have that much power over us, the latest women's magazine holds no sway because we have moved beyond comparisons, recognizing that we are loved precisely because we are unique, not in spite of it.

In his encyclical *God Is Love*, Pope Benedict XVI addressed the body obsession that has taken hold of our culture:

> Nowadays Christianity of the past is often criticized as having been opposed to the body; and it is quite true that tendencies of this sort have always existed. Yet the contemporary way of exalting the body is deceptive. *Eros*, reduced to pure "sex," has become a commodity, a mere "thing" to be bought and sold, or, rather, man himself becomes a commodity. This is hardly man's great "yes" to the body. On the contrary, he now considers his body and his sexuality as the purely material part of himself, to be used and exploited at will. . . . Here we are actually dealing with a debasement of the human body; no longer is it a vital expression of our whole being, but it is more or less relegated to the purely biological sphere. The apparent exaltation of the body can quickly turn into a hatred of bodiliness.[4]

That's what it comes down to. The body in today's culture has become a thing to be manipulated through diet and exercise, surgery and fashion, mainly for the purpose of attracting the opposite sex. It is no longer something to celebrate simply for the miraculous creation that it is, for a heart that pumps without any conscious effort on our part, for arms to comfort a child after a nightmare, for legs that carry us where we need to go. We tend not to see those glorious attributes behind the cellulite or spare tire. But they are there nonetheless, and we can't get from self-loathing to self-love without that realization.

Did you get stuck on the word "self-love"? Does it make you squirm a bit because it sounds too vain, too self-involved, too egotistical? We're not talking about vanity and self-absorption here. We're talking about a healthy love and acceptance of the person God created us to be. Jesus tells us: "Love your neighbor as yourself" (Mk 12:31). How can we love our neighbor if we can't or won't love ourselves, at least a little? When we hold ourselves to unrealistic standards, that perfectionist attitude can't help but trickle down. It becomes harder to have compassion for others if we have no compassion for ourselves.

So don't think of self-love as something opposed to your spiritual journey but rather something that will allow you to enter more fully into that Gospel call to love others as Jesus did. Look in the mirror right now, read the quote you taped there, think of yourself as loved beyond measure by God, and now imagine sharing that love with the people you live with, the people you work with, the people you meet in the store or on the street. What does this have to do with food? Nothing. And everything. It is only when we begin to love ourselves that we can begin to let go of the obsession to be someone else, look like someone else, act like someone else, live like someone else.

Live like you mean it. For this one day, don't worry about what you're going to have for dinner or how much you're going to weigh in the morning. That doesn't mean stuff yourself silly; just let go of the guilt and worry and obsession with food. Love yourself for who you are and begin to think about what you'd like to do now that you've freed up all that worry time. Make a list. Start to write down the things you've always wanted to do, a Bucket List of sorts. I did this not long ago and was surprised by some of the things that made their way onto my list, everything from catching up on doctor appointments that were long overdue to learning how to paint to writing some fiction to spending more time in nature. Weight loss or poor body image don't seem to have anything to do with those things, at least not on the surface. But when you dig a little deeper, you begin to see that a poor self-image makes us less likely to tackle something new, something that might call attention to us, when what we really want is to fade into the background.

Get your notebook and start your list today. Leave plenty of space to add to it over the coming weeks and months. Put down everything, even the things that seem outrageous or unlikely (for me that's a pilgrimage to Assisi), and begin to see yourself and your life as full of God-given possibility. List not only what you hope for but what you're thankful for, even the silliest or tiniest thing—the rain tapping on your roof, a full moon hanging in the sky, a child's giggle from another room. Sometimes, when we begin to look in unlikely places for the blessings around us, we are surprised to find our lives are already full to overflowing, and we no longer need food to fill us up. Trust what God has in store for you, no matter how things appear on the surface, or in the mirror.

Count Your Blessings

One of the stories that always comes to mind when I think about food, faith, and trust is the story of the feeding of the five thousand from Matthew 14:13–21. Jesus retreats to a deserted place after John the Baptist has been killed, but the crowds follow him. The disciples want Jesus to shoo the crowd away. "We have no food, only five loaves of bread and two fish," they tell him. "Bring them to me," Jesus says, and orders the crowd to sit. Suddenly there is enough bread and enough fish to go around, more than enough, enough extra to fill twelve wicker baskets. I love that image, baskets overflowing with food when earlier there was thought to be nothing.

In her book *Not Counting Women and Children*, Megan McKenna expands on the story for us and talks about the call to discipleship, which she says is "about risk, about letting go and giving over what we have on behalf of others' needs, about sharing and being the first to move toward others and about giving generously and blessing the gifts."[5] So much of what she says about this gospel reading connects to the journey we're on right now—the willingness to risk, to let go, to give over our fears.

McKenna talks about the gospel story of multiplication as it relates to Dorothy Day's Catholic Worker House in New York City, where a sign read: "Thank more and need less."

"Thank more, need less, eat less, share more, risk more, trust others, even strangers and crowds. Thanksgiving opens up a place inside us that changes emptiness to potency and possibility, that allows us to live more simply so that others may simply live," McKenna writes. "The disciples ate—but probably from the leftovers, when everyone was finished and full. We need to eat afterward, after the others are taken care of, satisfied. Then we can sit down with Jesus and eat the leftovers."[6]

Of course, the feeding of the five thousand ties in directly with Eucharist, where we are called to the table and given exactly what we need, no more, no less, just enough. The tiniest morsel of Eucharist is enough to satisfy our weary souls, reminding us that we do not need nourishment enough to fill twelve extra baskets; we need only enough to sustain us. Jesus fills us up not with plates heaped to overflowing, but with one host, one sip.

"Many people who struggle with food addictions and obsessions do so because they lack faith," says Cathy Adamkiewicz, a Michigan-based magazine editor who is also the mom of seven children and grandma to four, with number five on the way. "That sounds like a harsh statement, but I believe it's true. At the root for many of us is an inability to believe that we will be provided for; we don't trust. So many times I've looked at a delicious meal as if it's the last time I'll ever see wonderful food again. I can't believe that good things will be provided for me over and over again. At the very core of this dysfunction is my inability to fully trust God—God who provides for *all* of my needs."

Cathy told me that the Eucharist has played a role in her ability to heal her desire for unhealthy foods, whether it's a plate full of goodies or a bottle of wine.

"Whenever I go to Mass, I'm offered Jesus himself in the Eucharist. It's become a profound reminder that he will feed me—repeatedly. He is not capricious. He is always there, ready to give me exactly what I need. I don't have to 'stuff myself' spiritually; I can patiently wait for the Lord to provide for me just at the appropriate time," she explains. "This can transfer to my relationship with food. I know that there are many more special occasions coming in my life. This is not my last meal. There will be many good things for me each day. I have had to really give over this area to God, and to ask him to help me believe that he will give me good things in good time."

Cathy admits to a "scale addiction," weighing herself every day, sometimes several times a day, and allowing the number she sees to directly impact her outlook on life. The day we spoke the scale was down a pound or so, making her declare: "It's going to be a great day!"

"I have not conquered my scale addiction yet (although I've been known to give up weighing myself for Lent), but I have developed a spiritual practice that helps me take my eyes off the number. Affirmations may sound corny, but I've realized that what I tell myself has power. So whenever I get on a scale (at home or at my Weight Watchers weigh-in) I say out loud: 'It's just a piece of data.' That reminds me that we're talking about a number, a tiny fact in the whole picture," she says. "I know that I'm so much more than 'data.' One look at a crucifix reminds me that I'm a great deal more: He loved me so much that he was willing to die for me. He loves me just as I am."

Cathy's dieting odyssey began around age thirteen, when she wasn't even overweight. She found out some of her friends weighed less than her and so the quest for perfection according to someone else's standards began. She also remembers hearing her father tell her mother every day that she was fat. Her mother wasn't fat, Cathy stresses, but the message trickled down to Cathy anyway. Over the years she has tried all sorts of diet plans, and is currently having success with the slow and steady approach, replacing bad habits with healthy eating habits.

"For me, ultimately this is all about control. As a woman of faith, I know there is much more to it. I do have control of some things. I have free will, the ability to choose to trust God," she adds. "Ultimately I'm striving (not there yet!) to give this completely over to Jesus. I seek to abandon myself—my whole self, even my physical self—to his care. But of course it's scary. We are afraid of abandonment. We are afraid that we will lose ourselves. Of course, we know that in him we'll be freed. We just have to act as if we really believe that, and that's the tricky part."

Bigger than Both of Us

Clearly the food-faith connection is not a me-myself-and-I issue. We like to think our weight problems, our lack of self-esteem, our eating habits are really all about us, but they're bigger than that. It would be too easy to allow this to be a self-centered struggle, one where it's just us against our scale.

Our focus on the seeming lack in our lives seeps into our relationships at home and at work, our commitment to our community and our larger world, and our devotion to our prayer lives and journeys toward God. It's very hard to move forward if we are glued to an image or a number. We imagine we'll take the next step once we reach a certain weight or size, but we keep getting stuck, or, at the other end, moving the goal posts. The result is a constant unhappiness and unrest that prevents us from becoming who we are called to be: disciples willing to trust, risk, grow, and love.

Did you ever have that feeling of panic when you realize it's 4 p.m. and you still don't know what you're making for dinner that night? It happens at our house on a regular basis. We dig through the overstuffed freezer in our basement, through the two sets of pantry shelves downstairs and then the refrigerator and freezer upstairs. All are packed to overflowing, like those wicker baskets in the Gospel story. And still we decide we have nothing to make; another trip to the store is required.

"Thank more and need less." If that were our motto, we'd make a fabulous dinner from something already in our freezer and feel grateful for what we managed to make out of what seemed like nothing. But we buy more, need more, search for more. We are always hungry and never satisfied because we don't trust and we won't risk. Can we reach a place where we are satisfied with just enough?

You are enough. You have enough. Do not worry about tomorrow. God will provide in our lives just as God provides in the Eucharist. Let that be the message that plays in your head over and over from now on, as you shake off the chains of self-loathing and experience—maybe for the very first time—*la dolce vita*.

Food for Thought

1. Find a scripture verse, prayer, or inspirational quotation to hang on the mirror in your bathroom or bedroom. What quotation did you choose and why? How does it speak to you?

2. What is the negative tape that plays in your head? How long have you been hearing that message? What positive message reflecting God's love for you will you replace it with?

3. Was there an old photo that once made you cringe? Did you dig it out and look at it with fresh eyes? What was your reaction?

4. Read over your list of blessings and hopes. What stands out to you? Pick one thing you want to work toward and make that a priority. If it's a pie-in-the-sky plan, that's okay. Start by researching, reading, and putting some long-term goals in place.

5. Have you ever felt afraid you wouldn't have enough? What made you feel that way? Are there any connections between your fears and your eating habits? Where can you begin to trust more?

6. The next time you go up to receive the Eucharist, spend some time reflecting on how this sacred meal fills you up spiritually without filling you up physically. How do you feel about learning to be satisfied with "just enough," not too much, not too little?

7. Reflect on the motto "thank more and need less." How can you translate this into your own life? Make a list of ten things about yourself that you're thankful for that have nothing to do with your appearance or your self-image.

Practice

Allow yourself to eat one meal you really love with zero guilt. Savor every bite as a Roman would. Go out to a restaurant or prepare it at home. Eat slowly and with gusto. Invite family or friends to join you. Celebrate the blessing of good food shared with good friends. How does it make you feel to eat with abandon and not worry about the calories? Does it scare you? Does it feel like a dream come true, or does it make you feel out of control? Why?

Meditation

Comparisons get us nowhere,
and yet how often do we judge ourselves
not on our own merits and gifts
but on how we stack up against another.
It is a game we can never win.
Today we pray for the willingness
to let go of our need to live
according to the world's standards
and cling to God instead.
We praise you and thank you,
gracious Creator, for the blessings
that fill our lives to overflowing.

Chapter 4

Freedom by the Forkful

Breaking the chains of a high-fat, fast-food culture

Do you not know that your body
is a temple of the holy Spirit within you?
. . . Therefore glorify God in your body.
1 Corinthians 6:19–20

Barbara came from a big, loving, close-knit Irish Catholic family, one where she was encouraged and supported in everything she did. But she knew from early on that she had a "food thing" that set her apart from the rest of her family. She simply could not stop eating. She tried Weight Watchers three different times, diet pills, even a twenty-nine-day total fast in a hospital. No matter what she did, she always ended up eating the pounds back on.

At one point, she thought she had conquered her problem. After getting hooked on diet and exercise guru Richard Simmons's approach to weight loss, she took off one hundred pounds. She reveled in her newfound physical freedom and decided to go on a retreat, where she gave a talk about her weight-loss journey.

"I thought things were good. I thought I had it all figured out, but little by little the weight started coming back," she told me, remembering the day she saw a picture of herself and realized how much weight she had regained—ninety of the original hundred pounds.

Her best friend and roommate, Michele, posed an unlikely question regarding Barbara's diet struggle: How is your prayer life? Michele suspected what Barbara had not yet realized: There was a direct connection between her spiritual life and her physical issues.

"The religious part of it was always there for me, and looking back I realize that was my saving grace—having strong family and strong faith. After I gained all the weight back, I knew I had gotten to the point where it wasn't going to be a diet anymore. The diets would work if you stayed on them, but why couldn't I stay on one? It wasn't going to be a matter of a diet," Barbara recalls. "God started to weigh some things on my spirit that got me where I needed to be, like he was preparing me."

Barbara says she used to wonder why she was so different from everyone else. Other people seemed to like food as much as she did. They'd even pack on a few pounds during the holiday season, but then they'd take it right back off and be done with it. Not so for her. She added pounds and added pounds until her weight topped three hundred.

Her "Aha!" moment came one day when she was driving with a friend, who was in Alcoholics Anonymous. He casually mentioned that sugar is a drug for people who have food addictions.

"Most people might not want to hear that. For me it was like I realized there could really be something that's different about me. Maybe it's not just all psychological. Maybe I'm not just lazy or slothful or a glutton," says Barbara, who had tried Overeaters Anonymous ten years prior but says her spirit and her willingness weren't ready yet. "I still needed to walk the walk for another ten years and try to do it on my own," she says.

The second time at OA was a charm. It's been fifteen years, and Barbara has maintained the 150-pound weight loss that took her two years to achieve—even after the birth of her two children. But it's by no means an easy road to walk. She writes down everything she's going to eat every day, and she eats no sugar or flour products at all. Those physical elements are critical to her continued success, but equally important is the spiritual dimension.

"I have to work all three aspects—physical, spiritual, and emotional. As much as in my mind I don't want food to become my god, it will, because my body will take over," she explains.

Barbara says the spiritual dimension of her weight struggle really hit her when she was attending a retreat for people in 12-Step programs. The topic of "self-will" came up. She didn't think that term applied to her because she was "passive" and lacked confidence. But as she was driving home from that retreat, she experienced the full force of the self-will that had ruled her life until then. She was hungry and wanted to go to the grocery store immediately, before going home and having a healthy dinner. She knew it wasn't the right thing for her, but she was, as she explains, having an all-out "tantrum" in her car, refusing to do what she knew she needed to maintain her health.

"I realized that is self-will. I was having this internal battle with myself because I wanted to have my way, but I had to surrender to the fact that I needed to go home first. So I went home and ate, and my whole perspective changed," she says. "I have to work the physical part for the spiritual part to work. Otherwise I'll start convincing myself I need things that I don't really need."

The other turning point came after Barbara married and became pregnant with the first of her two babies. Although she still struggles with body issues—such as excess skin that sags from so much weight loss—having her babies has helped her learn to love her body as it is. "When my body did that the first time, I thought: 'This body that I've loathed my whole life, that I've never accepted, that people around me didn't seem to accept, and that society definitely did not accept, this miracle formed inside of it.' Once I started feeding my body healthy foods, my body did what it needed to do. God created my body to give life to these two babies. Even though I was over age forty-one before I was able to have them, it was a confirmation," Barbara says. "So I do have excess skin, but God brought me a wonderful husband for whom that's not an issue. I'm convinced that in his eyes I'm beautiful and it doesn't matter, so I don't really dwell on that because I know that's not really what life is about."

So what was the spiritual key for Barbara? Learning to trust God. She says that during that first hundred-pound weight loss, the loss that didn't stick, she *thought* she was trusting God. But it wasn't until she gave up the foods that spark her addiction that she realized she hadn't fully trusted or surrendered. She was still using food to fill herself up spiritually and emotionally, as well as physically.

"Food took care of my emotional needs. I didn't start dating till my mid- to late-thirties. I was fine with it because food just numbed me out. I went to church every Sunday, and taught in a Catholic school, but food was doing things for me that I didn't even realize it was doing," she explains. "When the food went away, I realized that when I say I trust God, I really have to trust him."

In true 12-Step form, Barbara takes her struggle one day at a time. It's the only way she can face a lifetime without sugar or flour in her diet and the hard work that entails.

"If I ask God to help me move a mountain, he's going to tell me to bring a shovel," she says, with a mischievous lilt in her voice. "I have to do the work. I can't expect to wake up and not have to do anything."

The Siren Song of Food

You don't have to have a food addiction to understand at least some of what Barbara has gone through in her lifetime, and what she continues to face each and every day. Our culture makes it so easy to fall into the high-fat, fast-food, supersize-me mentality that has resulted in unprecedented levels of obesity, even among young children. And, let's face it, most of us don't want to have to work hard at eating right or staying slim.

We probably all experience Barbara-like moments now and then, those times when we suddenly feel like we have to eat right now, even when we know that's not such a great idea. And so we pull up to the McDonald's drive-thru to order a shake and some fries or throw a family-size mac and cheese into the microwave, and thus fulfill our craving, give in to our "tantrum."

But what if, as Barbara has discovered, there's another way to look at things. What if we can get past our self-will to a place of surrender? We don't have to resort to the path of least resistance—the foods our kids will like most, the foods that are easiest to make, the foods that come in boxes and bags loaded with too many ingredients to count or pronounce. Surrender doesn't mean giving up; it means just the opposite—acceptance of and obedience to God's will regarding stewardship of our physical bodies.

When we slow down and begin to focus on our bodies as gifts from God, temples of the Holy Spirit, places worthy of care and attention and love, we begin to make choices that honor our bodies. We enter into our relationships with food in a whole new way. We stop seeing food as something to fill an urge or mask a need.

"I do see a connection between my desire to overeat and a deeper hunger for God, for my true self, and for my fullest potential. Food for me was a distraction so that I could avoid those spiritual hunger pains calling me to a deeper relationship with Christ," says Michael Scaperlanda, husband, father, grandfather, and law professor at the University of Oklahoma.

Michael recently took off sixty-five pounds he says had "accumulated over three decades." The day I contacted him, he had just posted a celebratory message on Facebook because he had reached that goal after twelve months of hard work. Looking back, he says he can see how his new eating plan has given him deeper insights into food and his spiritual life.

"As I have consumed less, I enjoy the food more and eat higher quality food—going from a one pound T-bone to a six-ounce filet for example—allowing me to taste and see the goodness of the food that God, through the work of human hands, has provided," he told me. "As I have grown to appreciate my food more, this has caused me to reflect on the divine food given to us in the Eucharist, drawing me closer to God."

"Since I wasn't 'dieting,' but instead attempting with God's help to correct a spiritual defect—gluttony—I hope it will be easier to keep the weight off," he added.

Nurturing the connection between body and soul starts us down a road less traveled, one where we crave healthier foods, slower mealtimes, more physical and spiritual space. From this new perspective, we willingly choose fewer mindless high-calorie fillers because we don't want to bog down our bodies and souls with things that wear us out, fatten us up, and lead to sluggishness and dissatisfaction and acedia, or inertia.

We can find magic in the moments of chopping, stirring, baking, eating, savoring, and sitting around a table and enjoying our food rather than standing at a counter eating directly from the bag. But that shift in attitude takes work, so get out your shovel and let's start digging.

Food writer Mark Bittman, in his book *The Food Matters Cookbook*, talks about the prevalence of unhealthy food in the American diet and the need to strip down and get back to basics. The problem is not just overconsumption of meats and trans fats and corn syrup and calories, he says. It's the cultural mindset that says we are willing to use an exorbitant amount of resources to produce things that aren't good for us or our children or our planet, things like diet soft drinks, for example.[1] On the surface, diet soda may seem like a "safe" food for people with weight issues, and yet it's part of a mindset that sets a course for yo-yo dieting and weight gain.

A recent study by the American Diabetes Association showed that those who drink diet soda most frequently, up to two cans a day, had waist circumference increases 500 percent greater than people who drank no diet soda. Although those figures may seem surprising at first glance, they are indicative of a larger, pervasive problem in our culture, a quick-fix mentality that makes us believe that drinking diet soda will somehow balance out our many other poor food choices.[2]

"Almost one-third of our total caloric intake comes from nutrient-poor foods like sweets, salty snacks, and fruit drinks. Soda alone accounts for a whopping 7 percent of our total daily calorie intake, with doughnuts, cheeseburgers, pizza, and potato chips not far behind," Bittman writes. "Incredibly, less than 6 percent of our calories come from unprocessed fruits and vegetables—perhaps the healthiest food group of all. And though manufacturers are in the process of rejigging junk food to reduce or eliminate trans fat (the solid form of vegetable oil that's worse for your heart than butter or lard) their products are still loaded with gratuitous oils and chemicals."[3]

Scan the shelves of your favorite grocery store. It isn't hard to find the culprits at eye level and at almost every turn. Over-processed convenience foods, ooey-gooey snack treats, even so-called "health foods" that are often nothing more than junk food in disguise, tempt us with their ease, their claims of being good for us, their promises of filling meals at cheap prices.

Bittman recommends what he calls "sane eating," which involves eating fewer animal products, eating all the plants you can manage, making legumes and whole grains a regular part of your diet, avoiding processed foods, and allowing treats—even daily—but within reason.

"Sane eating is about moderation, not deprivation, so feel free to eat the foods you'd miss, just in smaller portions and less frequently," he writes. "As long as you're making real changes in the way you eat most of the time, an indulgence every day is well deserved."[4]

Sane eating is the antidote to the diet mentality that has our culture in its grips, and Bittman's suggestions are far from novel. The monastics have been living moderation and balance for centuries, something we'll talk about in more detail in chapter 6. And other contemporary writers, Catholic and not, have long been touting the benefits of bringing some sanity to our overconsumption of food and just about everything else.

John Michael Talbot, the musician, author, and founder of the Franciscan Brothers and Sisters of Charity, talks about bringing our eating habits back to basics in his book *The Lessons of St. Francis: How to Bring Simplicity and Spirituality into Your Daily Life.*

"What's wrong with this picture? North Americans spend billions on lavish eating, on diets that contain too many harmful substances and too little of the necessary proteins and nutrients. Plus, we spend billions more on dieting pills, potions, and programs in an effort to escape the natural consequences of our consumption. In fact, we spend more on diet aids than the people of many nations spend on food,"[5] Talbot writes, adding that "balance and moderation" have been part of the Judeo-Christian tradition for thousands of years. He goes back to the book of Sirach to prove his point:

> Moderate eating ensures sound slumber
> And a clear mind next day on rising. . . .
> In whatever you do, be moderate,
> And no sickness will befall you. (Sir 31:20–22)

Like Bittman, he recommends bringing the daily diet back to some level of sanity by growing your own vegetables, when possible, or buying locally grown produce and locally raised eggs, meat, and milk, now known as the "locavore" movement. He also promotes a decrease in the consumption of animal protein and an increase in plant foods, and, finally, occasional fasting, which we will talk about in the next chapter.

You may have noticed by now that none of the food or spiritual "experts" recommend specific diets or calorie counts but rather over-arching principles to guide buying and eating habits. Learning to reclaim our bodies and our diets is not a matter of following someone else's diet plan but rather creating one of our own, one that fits our lifestyle, our health needs, our budget, our schedule, and our palate, with room for an occasional indulgence.

When was the last time you allowed yourself any indulgence without guilt? Imagine doing so regularly, and still keeping your weight and health in check. That's the happy byproduct of breaking out of the craving-diet-deprivation mentality. When we always feel deprived, we never feel satisfied, and when we never feel satisfied, we're always searching, seeking, and hungry, not for food but for peace and happiness. Every time we inevitably "slip" and go off our diets in an attempt to fill that deeper void, we feel guilty, and the vicious cycle begins again.

The Strength of Surrender

Becoming whole and holy requires us to move away from the microwave mentality toward something slow, basic, simple, real. It's the impetus behind the slow food movement, which attempts to reverse the fast food movement, as well as the locavore movement, organic movement, vegetarian movement, and all of the many other "movements" people today embrace in an effort to bring some meaning back to the mundane, to make their meals—and by extension their lives—less frantic and more full.

Stripping away to experience fullness: It's a paradox that mirrors so much of what we're discussing in this book, that seemingly opposite things are more than compatible; they are mutually beneficial. Body and soul, food and faith, simplicity and fullness. We have to move beyond the dualism our culture insists exists between these elements and rest in the connection that will allow us to become our truest, healthiest selves in every aspect of our lives. Finding and resting in that connection requires more than reading books and making home-cooked meals; it requires a deepening of our relationship with God, the source of all connection.

"Come to me, all you who labor and are burdened, and I will give you rest. Take my yoke upon you and learn from me, for I am meek and humble of heart; and you will find rest for your souls. For my yoke is easy, and my burden light," Jesus tells us in Matthew 11:28–30.

So often we are heavily burdened by this battle with food and weight and ego. So often we labor, or in this case, diet with no rest from the guilt and fear and restrictions we place on ourselves. There is little room for joy and peace and resting. Like Barbara, we diet and punish ourselves and lose weight, all the while thinking we are trusting God, when in truth we are holding on for dear life to all our misconceptions, the biggest among them being the belief that we have to do it on our own. We don't. We can't. We have to surrender, really surrender, to the One who holds the reins and will lead us where we need to go.

Think about the way we go to Mass and receive Communion. We don't pull up to a parish drive-thru window to receive the Body of Christ. We don't eat as we drive back home. We spend time preparing for the meal, praying as a community—candles lit, music playing, hands clasped, hearts open. The priest carefully prepares the table, laying out the vessels, gathering the ingredients from other members of the parish family, blessing our spiritual meal, and then, only then, inviting us to come up and mindfully, prayerfully, eat the Bread of Life and drink from the Cup of Salvation.

When we take our cues from our spiritual meal, we begin to see where we've dropped the ball at home. How often do we slowly and carefully prepare for a weeknight dinner? Do we set the table and gather the ingredients with focus and gratitude? Do we approach the preparations more as chore than opportunity, more as heavy burden than labor of love?

"In this culture, we have become so disconnected from nourishing our bodies, so disconnected from our food, from nature in general," says Deanna Beyer, a yoga teacher who practices the ancient art of Ayurveda, an Eastern practice which focuses on the connection between body and spirit, especially as it relates to food and eating habits.

Food is "consciousness," Beyer explains. In more modern terms: You are what you eat. If we constantly take in heavily processed, artificial, high-fat foods, we, too, become heavy—not just in body but in spirit.

"The standard American diet creates a sense of inertia. Fried foods, processed foods—they are so heavy, so manipulated. They are no longer the living, vibrant foods they once were," she says, adding that our bad food habits have become a poor substitute for what we're really searching for. "People wonder why they are so attached to feeding themselves these things. They are trying to give themselves love. Everyone is looking for a connection. What people don't realize is that one of our great fears is of being alone, that we are going through this process of being alive alone. We are never alone because we are all moving toward the same thing. Once you let go of that fear that you are in this alone, you can actually start to live a whole life, a more wholesome, happier life. That's big."

Beyer offers insights from Ayurveda that have the potential to transform our own food habits, even if we have no plans to take up the rather stringent principles of that practice. Food—from the buying to the cooking to the eating—can become something that brings light and life to our days rather than weight and guilt.

In what sounds like advice taken from the latest health magazine, she suggests buying and making the freshest food possible. But there's a twist. She says to try not to cook when you are angry or frustrated, but to prepare food with love, pouring joy and peace and kindness into the pot in much the same way we pour in water and spices.

"Infuse your food with a sense of gratitude and respect," says Beyer, adding that how we eat is even more important than what we eat. "We eat standing up, in the car, when we're doing other things. We try to multitask. We do things mindlessly, and we don't focus on the one thing we are doing," she says. "Sit down and look at your food. Give thanks to God for the nourishment you are taking in. Just taking the time to bless our food changes the whole way the food nourishes the body. It's not just that I am living to eat; I am eating to live and appreciating the fact that God has provided for us. There's a grand plan here, and nothing is by mistake."

Sounds a lot like what we do at Mass, doesn't it? We eat of Communion so that we may live. We bless our spiritual food, say, "Amen," and silently reflect on the significance of what we have just consumed not only into our bodies but into our hearts. It is possible to give our everyday meals a similar sense of the sacred, thereby transforming food from something that fills us up into something that truly nourishes.

As I mentioned in chapter 1, I have developed a morning breakfast routine that originally grew out of a silent retreat experience. At first it was a novel idea, something I did when I thought of it or when I had a few spare minutes, but over the years it has developed into a very specific spiritual practice, one that I miss if I'm unable to squeeze it in.

Every morning I wait until everyone has gone to work or school, at least on weekdays when we're on our "normal" schedule, before making my breakfast. I set out a placemat and a cloth napkin. I slowly and carefully measure my oatmeal into a bowl. And, yes, I use a microwave, proving that slow spiritual practices can fit into busy modern lives. As my food cooks, I get out a banana and peanut butter and light a small white candle in front of my place at the table. Then

I slice the banana, stir in the peanut butter, put all the containers and extra utensils away, and sit down at the table.

I look into my bowl and smell the wonderful combination of foods. I make the Sign of the Cross and bless my food, giving thanks not only for what I have to eat but for the new day ahead of me. I use the time before that first bite to pray for those who need my prayers, specific people who are sick or in need, as well as general intercessions. Then I take my first bite, savoring the textures and flavors, which seem so much stronger in the starkness of the silence and emptiness of the space around me.

Often, I'll feel my mind start to wander and worry about things on my schedule that day, so I call myself back to my oatmeal and try to focus on chewing and tasting and swallowing. It's not always an easy practice, when so many other things are calling for my attention, but it has given me an entirely new, and wholly peaceful, way to start my day. And now, rather than craving a bagel and cream cheese or a stack of pancakes, I crave this simple, basic, whole food and the simple, silent prayer that comes with it.

Food for Thought

1. What did you have for breakfast today? How did you make it? What did you do, if anything, while you ate it? Was it a peaceful or stressful meal?

2. Think about how you receive Communion when you go to Mass. What do you do as you prepare to go up to Communion? How do you receive? What are you reflecting on when you return to your seat?

3. How might you weave some of the practices from Mass into meals at home? Is there a time when you can try a silent meal?

4. If you don't already say a blessing before dinner each night, add this to your daily practice. Does it change mealtime? If so, how? What has been your family's reaction to this new practice?

5. Begin to take note of how you eat, not just at set mealtimes but throughout the day. Do you eat in your car? At the counter? At your computer? How do those meals satisfy you compared to meals taken slowly and quietly around a table with family or friends?

6. Can you begin to incorporate some "sane eating" principles into your life? Jot down some ways you can increase fruits and vegetables, decrease processed foods and meat, and even allow an occasional but reasonable indulgence. How realistic does that feel for you?

7. Have you, like Barbara, ever had a "tantrum" over something you felt you just had to have? What was it? Did you give in to "self-will" or resist?

8. Does the thought of surrendering your diet mentality scare you? If so, why? Think about how you might rely more on God and less on yourself for the changes you need to make.

Practice

Find a time when you can focus on meal preparations. Plan a healthy meal and then set about washing the vegetables, chopping, stirring, sautéing with full attention. As you prepare the vegetables or salad, meat or grains, think about where the food came from—the seeds, the farmers, the earth, the workers in the grocery store, the many blessings from God. As you chop or slice, turn the movement into meditation, focusing on each action. As you cook the food, pour love and gratitude into the pan along with the ingredients.

Set the table with care, choosing where people will sit and which favorite bowls you're going to use. Put a candle or some other special marker in the center of the table. Choose some soothing music to play in the background. Prepare for this everyday meal as if it were a special occasion. Make the steps leading up to the meal as important as the meal itself. Don't rush through anything or worry about what you have to do after the meal. Just focus completely on this one activity for this one meal.

How was this experience different from normal meal preparation for you? What did you like about it? What was difficult? Did it change the way you experienced your meal? Is there something you can take from this experience and incorporate into everyday preparations?

Meditation

We move through life
at breakneck speed,
never stopping long enough
to enjoy or even notice
the sights, the smells,
the tastes, the sounds
of the world all around us.
With each step, each breath
I take today, help me, God,
to savor things, big and small,
to drink in the gift of your presence
found in the most unlikely places.

Chapter 5

Feast or Famine

Changing attitudes toward how and why we eat

Eat food. Not too much. Mostly plants.
Michael Pollan

One of my favorite stories my ninety-nine-year-old grandmother, Helen, tells is of her younger days when she and my grandfather, Fred, and their cousins and other assorted relatives would get out of Brooklyn on a summer day for some time in the "country," which was anyplace where there was a big patch of grass with a grill of some sort for cooking.

"Once we were going on a picnic three hours away and we realized we forgot the tomato sauce, so we stopped and bought everything we needed and made sauce in a big pot on the grill. We had to boil the macaroni on the grill, too," my grandmother says, laughing as she remembers how my grandfather, obviously wise to the potential disaster in his midst, went off to find some twigs for kindling and didn't return until dinner was ready.

I love the image of my grandmother stirring up a fresh pot of tomato sauce on an outdoor fire in some upstate New York park back in the 1930s, and then tackling the even more daunting task of scrubbing what must have been blackened pots until they looked like new. The best most of us can muster during a camping trip or on-the-road picnic nowadays is to toss a few pre-packaged hot dogs and burgers on a propane grill or hibachi, maybe some fresh corn or baking potatoes if we're particularly ambitious. The more likely scenario is a trip through a drive-thru restaurant at a roadside rest stop or a hastily packed bag lunch eaten while in motion.

My grandmother's Italian immigrant family was not unlike most immigrant families back in the old days, and like many new immigrant families today. They kept the traditions of their homelands, especially when it came to food.

"We went crabbing a lot, and not with a net but with killie rings," my grandmother says, not realizing I don't even know enough to understand how much more difficult that method must have been for them. "Then we had to scoop them up. We made them into sauce or with garlic and oil, which everyone loved.

"My father made his own wine. I remember all the grapes coming, and my brother Joe was the one who stomped them," she continued, clearly enjoying this trip down her culinary memory lane. "And my sister Clara? She would put all those people you see on TV making macaroni to shame. She could whip pasta dough around like nothing."

My grandmother remembers canning jars of sauce and peppers and eggplant when it was in season, making "Easter pies" every Good Friday morning to break the Lenten fast on Holy Saturday, dipping delicate zucchini blossoms in batter and frying them until they were golden and lightly crisped.

"Now, forget it, people just go and buy a jar of something. It's getting to the point where people just go and buy everything already all cooked for them," she says, almost incredulous at the thought. "Today, Mary, it's altogether different."

You can't argue with a woman who's seen almost an entire century go by. She has had a front-row seat to some of the world's most dramatic events and changes, including changes to family mealtime, which is something verging on sacred for old-school Italians.

I can remember going to visit my relatives in Brooklyn, where dinners lasted all day and included not just a never-ending array of fresh pastas and cheeses, sauces and pastries, but laughter and loud conversation, guitar playing and card games. A Sunday dinner in Brooklyn was truly a feast in every sense of the word. And when my relatives came to visit us in the "country," the women would bring housedresses and little gold slippers so they could change out of their good clothes and jump into the cooking and cleaning fray. A family meal wasn't simply something you sat down and enjoyed for a few minutes; it was an all-day event, something to be savored, an opportunity for sharing stories as well as recipes and favorites dishes.

What happened along the way that shifted our society from hearty immigrants who spent hours making every last thing from scratch, right down to the wine, to frazzled families who rip open plastic and cardboard for nightly dinners timed by the minutes, sometimes seconds? Although there is some attempt among a growing number of Americans to return at least a little bit closer to the old days of fresh, homemade foods cooked slowly among family and friends, the sad fact is that it's simply not realistic for most of us to go without a microwave or prepackaged food long-term. You might as well ask us to cook tomato sauce over an open fire.

Food writer Jennifer Steinhauer, in an article in the *New York Times*, bemoans the fact that our penchant for taking the easy way out when it comes to cooking is showing up at bake sales and potlucks and other places where people used to like to showcase their kitchen skills. Where once homemade cookies and other sugary confections tempted bake sale buyers, now boxes of Dunkin' Munchkins and

store-bought cupcakes are dropped off and resold. Don't do it, Steinhauer begs, comparing the practice to buying socks at Macy's and
reselling them as your own handiwork at a craft fair.

"The more upscale the community for the bake sale, the fancier
the store-bought cookies. . . . Lower-income parents, especially first-
generation immigrants, often turn up at school parties with the best-
tasting homemade treats," she writes.[1]

There it is again, that reminder that food and diet are closely
associated with our ethnic ancestries, our families, our beliefs. Once
we start moving away from those core elements, we begin to lose
our connection to our food and, by extension, to a wholesome and
balanced way of eating and living.

Pass the (Homemade) Gravy

Our collective food habits have changed. There's just no getting
around that. But that doesn't mean we have to give up our individual
pursuit of something better, and better for us—real food, cooked at
home and shared around the kitchen table. It's simply a matter of
getting back to our roots, whatever those roots might be. If you don't
have food-related roots, it's time to create some.

Think back to your own family's food traditions, which so often
are intertwined with the traditions of faith. Chances are good that
many of your best and strongest memories come with smells and
tastes and images of vibrantly colored foods passed around a table
so crowded a second "kiddie" table was required. Perhaps you can't
go home again, but you can begin to weave elements of those good
old-fashioned meals into your modern fast-paced life.

Cardinal Timothy Dolan of New York has made family meals one
of his crusades, writing about it on his blog and in his weekly column,
"Lord, to Whom Shall We Go," in *Catholic New York* newspaper. He

considers the communal meal critical to strong families, healthy children, and overall happiness.

"Yes, you heard me: if a family has a meal together regularly, as often as possible, at least two or three times a week, the members of that family have happier, healthier (and, by the way, holier) lives," he wrote in his September 23, 2010, column.[2]

Dolan went on to challenge Catholics to get back to this basic family meal at least once a week, reminding us that this physical mealtime is tied so closely to our weekly spiritual meal: "I guess we Catholics should hardly be surprised at all by all of this. Most of us fifty and over can recall that supper together as a family was rather routine and taken for granted, with Sunday dinner the most significant. We know as well that the Sunday meal—the Mass—of our supernatural family, the Church, is indispensable for our fidelity to Jesus and his Church. We Catholics also belong to cherished ethnic backgrounds, which celebrated every Sunday, holiday, holy day and important life event—baptisms, first Communions, birthdays, marriages, even deaths—with family meals," he wrote. "Our parishes, schools and programs need to get behind what should be a national crusade; let's start sitting down for a family meal as regularly as possible.

"In a world stuffed with complex issues, there is at least one easy answer!"[3] Many of us read that and think, "What's so easy about sitting everyone down to a family meal?" The teenager has Boy Scouts, the tween has soccer, the six-year-old has ballet class, and that's before we begin to factor in back-to-school nights, school board meetings, and all the other commitments that vie for our attention. But the cardinal speaks the truth, as do many other experts who promote family mealtime as the key to a saner and happier home life. To top it off, it's also the key to a saner and healthier diet.

If you begin eating more meals at home, whether on your own or with your family, you move away from the drive-thru mentality. You're no longer eating leftover Chinese right from the carton as you stand at the counter and sort the mail before you fly out the door to pick up one of the kids. Family mealtime forces you to slow down, even if it's just a little bit, and slowing down is always an important part of putting food and diet in perspective and on track. Because when we do things slowly, more mindfully, we become aware, and when we become aware we no longer want to shovel food in. We want to appreciate every bite, and that has multiple benefits. Yes, it strengthens family bonds, but slowing down also aids weight loss and improves health.

In a study of over three thousand men and women in Japan, for example, it was clear that "eating until full and eating quickly are associated with being overweight" and that the combination of the two habits—eating until full and eating quickly—"may have a substantial impact on being overweight." In another study, researchers at the University of Rhode Island gave thirty college-aged women large plates of pasta and told them to eat as much as they wanted. The amount of calories they consumed dropped significantly when they were told to slow down and chew their food a minimum of fifteen to twenty times. Aside from the obvious—that eating more slowly would naturally mean consuming few calories per minute—there's another bonus to this approach to eating. It takes between ten and forty-five minutes for the body to recognize that it's full, so the slower we eat, the more likely we will feel full before we get to the point of overeating.[4]

At our house, as crazy as it can get at times, I attempt to cook homemade meals most nights of the week with fresh vegetables and lots of whole grains, and I always make homemade tomato sauce. You can probably imagine what my grandmother would say if I didn't. I recreate my mother's Irish soda bread every St. Patrick's Day and her bread stuffing every Thanksgiving. I still cook seafood on Christmas Eve, in deference to my Italian heritage, and can stuff an artichoke like nobody's business. I'll even venture out into the traditions of other cultures and faiths—latkes during Chanukah or enchiladas on Cinco de Mayo.

Of course, not every night can be a feast, nor should it be. And therein lies the problem. Our culture tries to convince us on just about every front that more is better. More is a sign of wealth, luxury, power. Gone are the days when meals were moments of connection and conversation; now it's all about consumption and calories.

I can go to my upstate New York grocery store in mid-December and pick up fresh strawberries and mangoes, figs and kumquats. I don't need to wait for a certain season, a specific holiday, or any day at all. I can buy anything I want and eat it right away. Although it seems fabulous, some may say necessary, to have access to just about every kind of food any day of the week, with that access comes an undercurrent of constant feasting. We're disappointed if every meal isn't an event.

Sometimes, when one of my children is staring into the pantry or refrigerator bemoaning the fact that he or she can't figure out which of the many breakfast options to pick, I will remind them that not every breakfast needs to be something worthy of posting to a food blog. Sometimes food is simply fuel, something we eat to live. But with TV ads and billboards and in-store displays saying otherwise— in colorful and provocative ways—that can be a hard case to make.

Being able to serve whatever we want, whenever we want, and as much as we want has become the American way, a sign that we have arrived. But having unlimited choices of everything from produce to Pop Tarts to pudding hasn't made our diet better. In fact, too many options may have had the exact opposite effect.

"I have patients who go to Walmart and crumble in the cereal aisle because there are too many choices," says Lilly Casscles, a clinical psychologist based in upstate New York. "It's ridiculous. No wonder we feel so disconnected. We are surrounded by way too much, and it becomes overwhelming."

Lilly, who has her own struggles with weight issues, says our culture's obsession with food and diet is "insane" to people who have known what it's like not to have enough food at some point in their lives. She tells her patients battling food or weight issues to look at their parents, aunts and uncles, and grandparents for a healthy perspective. Most didn't diet or need to make special arrangements to be physically active. Their everyday lives were already active and food just took its natural place.

"We have lost sight of the fact that it is such a luxury to be so obsessed with diet and exercise, and to have so many obese poor people," says Lilly, adding that the way to make weight and diet changes stick is to avoid the fads and go for a simpler and perhaps more old-fashioned approach. "Modest changes to diet and activity levels over long periods of time will give you the most bang for your buck."

We don't like to hear that. We want the quick fix. The diet that focuses on a miracle food, the pill we can pop, the piece of exercise equipment that promises fat will melt away. Slow and steady isn't very glamorous, or popular. But that simple advice is totally in keeping with what health experts and spiritual guides would say. Diet, exercise, prayer—no matter what "improvement" we're trying to make, it requires not just a one-week or one-month program but a total change of perspective.

The Flip Side of the Feast

Clearly we need to break free of the feast-first, feast-always attitude of the world around us and seek out something more balanced. Throughout history, faith and ethnic cultures have provided us with a framework for sane and healthy eating, but modern society has twisted those traditions into something that serves the secular party-all-the-time mantra. You need look no further than Mardi Gras, Fat Tuesday, to see what I mean.

Back in the day, Fat Tuesday, or Shrove Tuesday, was a time to use up those foods that could not be eaten during Lent—sugar, fat, dairy, eggs. The night before Ash Wednesday, the faithful would dine on pancakes and breads and pastries that would be off-limits for the next forty days. It was a feast before the fast. Today, however, Mardi Gras is a celebration unto itself. Most revelers have no intention of fasting throughout Lent, and even those who do fast probably stick to Fridays without meat or some other small sacrifice. So we are left with a feast with no real meaning, other than to provide us with one more excuse to eat with abandon.

For Jeff Young, known as "The Catholic Foodie" for his blog and podcast of the same name, Mardi Gras isn't a day but a season. And, being from southern Louisiana, he knows how to get into the true spirit of things. He kicks off Mardi Gras season with his first King Cake on the Feast of the Epiphany and follows it up with a King Cake every week until Lent begins. That's a lot of cake. In the last twelve days before Fat Tuesday, Jeff and his family hit several of the major Mardi Gras parades. The festivities culminate with a pig roast or, as he says, a *cochon de lait*, for eighty to a hundred of his closest friends.

"Unfortunately, Mardi Gras is an example of a Catholic celebration that has been usurped and commercialized by mainstream businesses and media companies—MTV, Budweiser, Playboy, etc. Many people across the country think of the bawdy things that happen on Bourbon Street when they hear the words 'Mardi Gras,' but Bourbon Street is only one street, in one city, in one state," he says. "Mardi Gras is huge down here. It's not just on Bourbon Street. And it's a family event."

As much as Mardi Gras is a Catholic celebration with deep cultural roots in Louisiana, so is Lent. Jeff told me that in New Orleans, where Catholic churches on just about every corner sponsor fish fries every Friday night, even Protestants abstain from meat on Fridays.

"I know that's not much of a sacrifice, but *everybody* knows it's Lent, and everybody knows you're supposed to give something up. So at least our cultural Catholicism keeps Lent in the forefront of everybody's mind," says Jeff, who switches from baking King Cakes to making pretzels once the Lenten season begins. On fast days, he and his family have only a couple of pretzels for lunch and a couple more for dinner, a stark contrast to the weeks before, which is how the feast-fast routine was originally intended to work. But in our culture, very few trade in the revelry of Mardi Gras for the asceticism of Lent.

We have come to associate "fasting" as some sort of outdated punishment that no longer applies to us, a penance we don't need to serve. But fasting, when approached from a place of faith, can have far-reaching positive implications for both our physical and spiritual well-beings.

"Food is an obsession in our culture, and I really think we need wisdom from the Church about eating," said Msgr. Charles M. Murphy, author of *The Spirituality of Fasting: Rediscovering a Christian Practice*. "It's a basic human activity and there is wisdom in this whole tradition of fasting, which is focused on God and not on ourselves."

Fasting can be found throughout scripture, in the earliest Christian communities, in the lives of the Desert Fathers, and the writings of the Church Fathers. It has a long history because it's effective, which would account for its presence in the practices of so many of the world's great religions. Buddhists, Hindus, Jews, and Muslims all have fasting elements in their spiritual exercises.

Remember, when we're talking about fasting, we're not referring to the kind of diet fasting we do the morning after we've had a few too many slices of pie on Thanksgiving. Fasting requires an underpinning of prayer to prevent it from morphing into a diet designed to make us more appealing by worldly standards, not godly standards. Fasting is not an effort to lose weight; it is an act of humility before God. And that simple act can open us up in ways we never imagined.

"It's creating an empty space for God to fill. It's also penitential; it's an expression of our desire to be converted from sin and selfishness," Msgr. Murphy said, explaining that the Catholic tradition of fasting isn't a sign that we hate food. "We're not against feasting. In fact, we fast in order to feast better, to enjoy our feast."

There are several kinds of fasting—total, where we don't eat at all for a set period of time; partial, where we may fast for a portion of the day or for certain meals; and penitential, where we fast for a set time or give up certain foods, habits, or behaviors to undo some of our sinful or errant ways. During Lent, fasting takes center stage as one of the "three pillars" of this solemn and holy season, alongside prayer and almsgiving. The three work together supporting and expanding each other.

Fasting, in the Catholic sense, takes what might otherwise be a diet and gives it the direction and motivation needed to become truly life-changing and, when practiced regularly, potentially world-changing. When we fast in solidarity with those who are hungry, for example, and connect ourselves to others through prayer, we begin to take diet out of the kitchen and into the world at large.

According to St. Augustine, prayer and fasting are the "two wings of charity." In other words, our efforts to bring about positive change in our world are aided by our ability to pray and fast. It may be hard for most of us, with our limited fasting experience, to see how giving up a meal or favorite food or beverage could possibly cause a ripple effect of goodwill. It's not so much that my skipping a sandwich at lunch will provide relief to a hungry child across the globe, but that it will open my eyes—and my belly—to the sufferings of those who go without on a regular basis. When I take the money I might have spent on a meal or treat and donate it to the poor, I take that connection even further.

The emptiness fasting creates will make us more aware of the injustices in the world and of our own comforts and supposed "needs." Think of how often we say, "I'm starving." Or, I "need" a cup of coffee, piece of chocolate, glass of wine, handful of nuts. Fasting helps us begin to distinguish between wants and needs, even when practiced in the most minimal ways.

Margaret Miles, former dean of the Graduate Theological Union at Berkeley and author of *Desire and Delight: A New Reading of Augustine's* Confessions, recommends limited fasting as a way to put us back in touch with our food, our bodies, and our lives.

"Even a small experiment like skipping one meal is enough to demonstrate to most of us the degree to which we have become addicted to food, not only as our bodies require and enjoy it, but also for organizing our days. One day's worth of fasting will demonstrate an astonishingly different experience of time during that day," Miles wrote in an article in *Christian Century*.[5]

"Breaking our eating patterns, even briefly, both teaches us the psychological dimension of our attachment to food and to mealtimes, and loosens that attachment so that it never again has quite the strength that it had when we were not conscious of it," she adds. "Fasting is also good for the body; short fasts lasting from one to three days allow it to rest from its constant labor of digestion."[6]

No one should undertake a day-long fast—or anything longer—without checking with a doctor first. But certainly small forays into true Christian fasting coupled with prayer can, indeed, break us out of our routines and make us see what we may not have been willing to see before.

Last Lent, I decided to give up in-between-meal eating and to fast every Friday until dinner, which was vegan since I'm already vegetarian and wouldn't be giving anything up if I simply skipped meat. Because the practice was linked to prayer and to the liturgical life of the Church, I was able to stick with my self-imposed sacrifice. It was so successful, in fact, and brought so much depth to my prayer life, as well as my active life, that I decided to continue the practice after Lent was over. Easter Monday arrived and I muddled through, feeling deprived for the first time in forty days. Somehow what I did so willingly and so easily during Lent began to feel like a real imposition. I didn't make it three days before I was back to my old ways of snacking between meals and eating normally on Fridays. I knew the reason. During Lent, my fast was part of my sacrifice in solidarity with the poor and in reparation for my own shortcomings. When I lost my Lenten focus and didn't replace it with another prayerful intention, the practice was no better than a diet and it failed just as quickly as any other passing fad might.

If you came of age before Vatican II, you may remember fasting from midnight until you received Communion at Mass the next day. Now you can eat waffles at nine a.m. and receive Communion at the ten a.m. Mass, no fasting to speak of there. Older Catholics may even remember what are known as Ember Days, seasonal times of fasting.

At the start of each season, Catholics would fast on a Wednesday, Friday, and Saturday—chosen because they corresponded to the days of Christ's betrayal, crucifixion, and entombment. These special days, adapted from pagan practices, mirrored what other faiths continue to do, reminding us that we can transform the feast-or-famine approach to dieting into something with the potential to transform us from the inside out.

"After a single day of voluntary deprivation, a strange new connection had been forged between flesh and spirit," writes Paula Huston in *The Holy Way*. "The body itself had seemingly done what it always did: demanded to be fed as soon as it felt the pangs of hunger. My deliberate choice not to respond to it, and the fact that my body had survived just fine—in fact, had been surprisingly acquiescent about the whole thing—was a big clue that the hunger I so dreaded was probably not even centered there, but somewhere else entirely."[7]

And that thought brings us full circle, back to the need, the desire to be constantly feasting, not because we are hungry for food but because we are hungry for something more—God, acceptance, love, success, whatever it is that is clamoring outside our souls waiting to be let in. By learning to balance the feasts and the fasts, by finding a moderate middle road, by making the time and space to eat—or not eat—with peace and prayerfulness, we open the door just a bit and God comes rushing in.

Food for Thought

1. Did your family have any food traditions for holidays or other special occasions? What do you remember most about them? Have you continued those traditions?

2. How often do you share family meals at home? What makes your meals more stressful? What brings a sense of calm to dinnertime?

3. Describe your favorite mealtime memory in detail. Include smells, tastes, images, snippets of conversation you may remember. What makes that memory so special?

4. Have you fallen victim to the feast-always mentality of our culture? Do you find yourself feeling deprived if every meal isn't something special? Begin to think about ways to bring more simplicity and sanity to those meals.

5. Are there any popular diet practices that you've tried or considered —vegetarian, locavore, organic, slow food? If so, how have the strategies worked for you? What was good? Bad?

6. Do you practice fasting during Lent or any other time? What kind of fasting? How do you incorporate prayer into the fasting? What results have you seen from this practice?

7. How do you see your physical life connected to your spiritual life? Do you think tending to one affects the other? If so, how? Do you have any physical practices—other than fasting—that have improved your spiritual life, or vice versa? Talk about them now.

Practice

In keeping with the Sabbath and old-fashioned traditions, set aside a Sunday afternoon for a special meal. Maybe even pull something out of your family's recipe book. Eat in the dining room, if you have one; use your best dishes; carefully plan the menu; involve family and friends in the preparation; and be sure to say a blessing before you eat. Make it a true feast, not just of food but also of faith and friendship and family. Consider renewing the tradition of Sunday dinner in your family, if not every week then once a month. Invite extended family when possible, and watch how your own family blossoms as new ties are forged and strengthened.

In the week that follows your initial Sunday feast, pick a day when you will do some sort of fast. Perhaps eat only one full meal that day, as you would on a fast day during Lent. Or give up in-between-meal eating if that's something you do regularly. If you can't do any serious fasting just yet, find some small sacrifice—giving up sweets, skipping meat, forgoing your nightly glass of wine. Link whatever fasting you do to prayer, perhaps setting an intention for your fast, praying for particular people in your life or in solidarity with those who are hungry. At the end of the week, contemplate the results of your feasting and fasting.

Meditation

So much of life
is out of balance today.
Too much, too little,
too caught up in the whirlwind.
The world insists we need
more, more, more, more,
pushing us to grab all we can.
But wait. Slow down. Stop.
There is another way,
a better way, the only way.
Only by emptying ourselves out
before God will we find
fullness within ourselves.

Chapter 6
Balancing Act
Cues from the monastics

Food should be treated with respect,
since our Lord left himself to us in the guise of food.
Dorothy Day

If your house is anything like ours—and I'm kind of selfishly hoping it is—the clutter and chaos often hover just below circus level, and meals are no exception. Try as we might to maintain some semblance of sanity and, dare I say, serenity during nightly dinners or weekend breakfasts, the end result is usually noise, noise, noise, with occasional sibling bickering and complaints about the food thrown in for good measure.

For years, when the kids were younger, I would read parenting books, food magazines, and spiritual classics in hopes of calming our crazy dinner scene, which is why I jumped at the chance to see the movie *Into Great Silence* when it came out a few years back. The 162-minute almost-silent film about the Carthusian monks in the French Alps was a chance for me to experience vicariously the peaceful kind of meal I couldn't find around my own dinner table. As if that weren't enough, I figured I'd pick up some helpful hints on bringing the monastery atmosphere back to my home. On the big screen I found much of the calming beauty I had expected to see: one monk silently, rhythmically chopped celery; another worked in the garden; yet another wheeled a cart of covered dishes to monks in their individuals "cells." Simple meals of soup and bread were eaten silently, prayerfully, in front of a window looking out at the snow-covered Alps. No wonder these monks are so peaceful.

Later in the film, I got a glimpse of the monks' weekly communal meal, eaten together in the refectory in order to have a "family experience." In the silence of the sparsely populated movie theater, I laughed out loud. Clearly the monks' notion of a family dining experience was as far off-base as my notion of monastic life. There was no one whining that he didn't like kale. There was no one standing on a chair begging for waffles instead of soup. There was no one sulking at the end of the table because he couldn't cut his food.

In that moment, I came to the sudden realization that while those of us living out in the world can learn a lot from the monastics about praying, eating, and living in general, we are not and never will be monks. And so we must learn to take the best of what they have to teach us and adapt it to our busy and typically noisy home lives. It's not an easy task, I know, but by taking our cues from monastic life, we can discover a rhythm, a balance, and a peacefulness that has the potential to transform not only our mealtimes but our very lives.

The Rule of St. Benedict and the traditions of monastic communities through the centuries and up to the present day value healthy and moderate eating and drinking. Monks and nuns, with their focus on freshly grown foods cooked according to season, are the originators of the slow-food, locavore style of growing, buying, cooking, and eating that has become a contemporary fad. From the choice of food and eating environment to the rhythm of the days and seasons, monastics can teach us how to feed ourselves in ways that add to our spiritual growth and physical health rather than detract from them.

Brother Victor-Antoine d'Avila-Latourrette, in his bestselling cookbook *Simplicity from a Monastery Kitchen*, talks about the centrality of food in the monastic traditions of world religions—Hindus, Buddhists, and others, as well as Christians. But for Christians, the significance of food takes on greater meaning because of its inherent connection to our ultimate spiritual food, the Eucharist.

"The daily rhythm of monastic life attaches great importance to the time spent in the kitchen and food preparation, to time in the refectory and the act of consuming food. Saint Benedict attached great importance to these matters, and throughout the whole of monastic tradition, food retained a sacred character because of the importance given to it by Christ himself," Brother Victor-Antoine writes. "Anyone participating today in the life of a monastery notices the importance the monks and nuns give to their meals, their practical and healthy method of cooking, and their reverential way of serving food at the table and their equally reverent consumption of it."[1]

Serenity in Simplicity

If you flip through Brother Victor's vast array of monastery cookbooks, it will become readily apparent that while food is important to monastic life, it is not necessarily served in large quantities or with lots of complicated sauces and ingredients. Simplicity. That is the key. Tasting the food you're eating as opposed to smothering it in butter or sauce or salt or some other condiment. Fresh food, cooked simply and served with care. Even the busiest person can probably manage that. Dried lentils and vine-ripened tomatoes, local cheeses and farm fresh eggs, earthy mushrooms, bright green escarole, warming soups. Almost every recipe in the *Simplicity* book fits onto one small page, ingredients, instructions, and all. Simplify, simplify. That is our man-tra as we begin to follow a monastic way of giving food an important but healthy place in our days and lives.

When I went on retreat recently to the Kripalu yoga center in Lenox, Massachusetts, I had been warned (in a good way) that the mostly vegetarian food would be phenomenal, so phenomenal, in fact, that I was likely to overeat and feel uncomfortable, especially when it was time to move into downward dog or shoulder stand.

I stood before the long line of steam trays filled to the rim with healthy salads and soups, organic casseroles and braised tofu, veg-gies and homemade breads. Even the breakfast buffet boggled the mind with the bounty of hot cereals, eggs, muffins, nuts, and cooked fruit. By the middle of day two I was feeling the effects of this health food feast, so I took a stroll over to the "basics bar," a separate buffet where the food is stripped down. Vegetables are simply steamed; rice is white and plain; soups are clear and mostly broth; rice cakes fill in for muffins and breads. There is a recognition at this super-health conscious locale that even the healthiest, freshest foods can become too much if we overdo it day after day. Our meals need to be basic most of the time, feasts only on occasion, which stands in opposition to our American attitude of feasting whenever possible, even during a weekday lunch hour.

I will actually crave steamed broccoli when I eat too much heavy food. Suddenly a plate of bright green stalks seems as mouthwater-ing as ice cream, and nothing else will do. It's not that I'm on some higher food plane, but that I've developed a willingness to listen to my body, something that's grown out of years of being a vegetarian, doing yoga, jogging regularly, and trying to eat well enough to avoid the colon cancer that claimed my mother at age forty-seven. Of course, sometimes I hear what my body wants and ignore it, but most of the time I listen because, when it comes down to it, my body really does know what it wants and needs. And what it wants and needs is not one more trip to the Dunkin' Donuts drive-thru.

The craving for simple, fresh food is something we can all cultivate within ourselves through awareness, prayer, mindfulness, and plain old common sense, and the monastics are just the ones to get us started on the journey.

Building a Balance

I called Brother Victor for some pointers. On a cold winter day, he answered the phone at Our Lady of the Resurrection Monastery in Millbrook, New York, where he lives under the Rule of St. Benedict. He told me he needed to check on something in the kitchen before we could talk. I smiled as I realized I was listening to the pages of his cookbook world come to life.

Although our society seems more and more disconnected from the food that reaches our tables, Brother Victor says he sees dramatic positive signs that people are starting to recognize what the monks have known all along: You can be frugal and still eat fresh and delicious food in a way that not only sustains the body but the mind and soul as well, not to mention the local farming community.

"We try to live healthy lives and we try to be frugal. Basically we are vegetarian; we don't eat much meat. We try to keep the balance that St. Benedict wrote about in his Rule. He said to have balance in all things. It's a question of eating what you need for sustaining yourself but not going beyond that. It's a way of wisdom," he said. "There's a great return to eating locally. That's what we have been doing all along, but it's being rediscovered with new richness."

Brother Victor stresses that for Catholics especially there is a "very good biblical basis for the appreciation of food" that should encourage us in our own healthy appreciation. "In the Gospel, we read that Jesus, the Son of Man, came eating and drinking. He did have an appreciation for food and moderate drink, to the point that, as Dorothy Day said in one of her quotes, he leaves his Body and Blood under the auspices of food and drink, so it's sacramental. There's such a basis in our theology for appreciation of food and drink in light of what Christ himself lived and taught. You can expand from there," he explained. "And we get good principles from St. Benedict as well: Balance in all things. You keep a certain sense of moderation."

As much as the monastics live a balanced life, they also live a life set to a spiritual rhythm—the rhythm of the seasons and the rhythm of the liturgical year. "So much of our food follows the same pattern as what is available in season and what is being served during Lent or Advent or Christmas, for example. You see how something as basic as food is incorporated into daily monastic life by living in harmony with the seasons, both of nature and the liturgy," Brother Victor said, adding that modern-day families can create their own versions of the balance and harmony found in monastic meals without much effort.

"It's a question of priorities, a question of simplicity of life. There's no reason for at least one meal, the evening meal, people can't make a dinner. It may take only forty-five minutes to an hour. It's time well spent. It's something that will pay off later with profits for your health and your family," he told me, adding that it helps if parents can involve the whole family in the preparation.

"Make preparing food an enjoyable time. People can get into it and learn the value of these different elements, how to balance a meal. It's not just a question of eating and filling ourselves up and then just forgetting. Making food is something that can really bring quality into your own personal life and your family, not only on feast days or special occasions. Do it as an everyday thing, even if it's in a simpler form, and then perhaps on weekends or feast days you do something more elaborate," he urges, stressing that, just as in monastic life, mealtime for families is about creating community. "It's a time for coming together and meeting and becoming one mind and one soul like the Acts of Apostles says. That's what meals meant to the early Christians. It's something that has to be recuperated in our culture. It's difficult because our lives are so compartmentalized now and people are going in different directions."

Back when he was growing up in France, Brother Victor would eat at his grandparents' house every Sunday afternoon. Everyone was there, he said—aunts and uncles and cousins. It brought people together. Anyone who knocked on the door was invited in, in much the same way the Benedictine monks focus on hospitality and receiving every person as if they are receiving Christ himself. Although families are dispersed across the country now, it's important for those who are able to make an effort to eat together and create special meals.

"People are hungry for spiritual food. They're hungry for material food and for what nourishes mind, soul, and body. There needs to be unity," he said, explaining that unity is the reason behind the monastery practice of having a spiritual reading during a meal. The monks are feeding body, mind, and soul all at once.

Brother Victor suggests families try to incorporate some spiritual reading at least during the seasons of Advent and Lent, or, if nothing else, put on spiritual music for inspiration and contemplation during mealtime now and then.

"When people come on retreat, we read something and then put a CD on. They learn to appreciate that, eating in a contemplative setting, with a contemplative attitude," he told me. "Even during the preparation of food, some quiet enhances the food preparation. It brings harmony, intuition. We approach the food with an attitude that's reverent. Christ had such reverence for food."

Finding Your Rhythm

Michelle Francl-Donnay is a chemistry professor and spiritual writer who has experienced that quiet reverence that can be found—or cultivated—when preparing a meal. In one of her monthly columns for the *Catholic Standard & Times* of Philadelphia, she writes about making a pot of soup in an effort to get out from under the dark cloud gathering over her work and prayer life:

> Unable to escape to warmer climes or a hermit's cell, on a bitter cold Friday, I found myself making soup. Soup demands my full attention, perfection is forced to take a back seat to completion—driving off the demons of demand. Heaps of roughly cut vegetables grew on the cutting board, then were cast into the pot. One layer followed the next, the flavors intensifying in the confines of the pot. The individual chunks finally surrendered to the blender, and what had thirty minutes previously been unscrubbed carrots and onions buried in the vegetable crisper were gloriously whole and sustaining. I filled my bowl, to find I was no longer hungry. The mere act of making the soup had left me fed.[2]

I understand exactly what Brother Victor and Michelle are saying. For me, preparing a meal, chopping the vegetables, stirring a sauce, even steeping tea can provide more satisfaction than the food itself. I find that when I make a pot of coffee in the coffee maker, I throw it together, pour it, and drink it on the go. Sometime I turn the coffee-maker on only to realize an hour later that I completely forgot about it. But when I decide to make a cup of tea, the ritual involved slows it down to something more satisfying than simply a hot drink. I boil the water, pick out a particular type of tea, slice a lemon, drizzle some honey, steep it all in the two-handled monk mug that my husband gave me one Christmas, and then sit with hands cupped around the warm mug while I breathe in the sweet-smelling steam. I don't have to take a sip for the tea to begin to calm my soul even before it soothes my throat or fills my belly.

How we prepare our food, how we consume our food really makes a difference in how our food satisfies us and shapes the role we give food in our lives. Is it something we stuff in to satisfy an urge or something we savor to feed us physically and sustain us spiritually?

Michelle told me she not only focuses on how she prepares and cooks her food but also on seemingly insignificant things, like how the table is set, what dishes are used, and how and where people are seated. (And she doesn't allow electronics, books, TV, radio, or phone calls during dinner at home.)

"I was reading a piece on time management, in which a twenty-something guy talked about how he found fifteen extra hours a week by hiring someone to cook for him. What I found sad about it was that he said he saved even more time by eating directly out of the Tupperware containers that the cook left his dinner in," she said. "Somehow, even when eating alone, I want to set the time apart by using 'real' dishes—even in my office at the college, and definitely when I'm at home."

Even Michelle's children have picked up on her philosophy that eating is something to be done with care and joy. When her son lost a bet with a friend (a bet that he wouldn't get into Georgetown, which happily he did), he paid up by baking a chocolate cake and taking it to his friend on one of Michelle's best cake plates, something that many moms might not appreciate.

"I love that he used it, and that he would send it out freely, and not think he can't touch the good stuff. Somehow using those things feels like an act of generosity. It says to me that I'm not worried about breaking things; I'm instead focused on the joy of those who get to use them—and often the people that gave me particular things," Michelle told me. "I think we can bring some of the monastic traditions into our homes by attending to what we eat, even if it is simple, to surround eating by a bit of ritual, and in so doing slow things down a bit, by welcoming everyone's help in the preparation of the food. St. Benedict's Rule calls for everyone to take a turn working in the kitchen."

Clearing the Clutter, Calories, Confusion

If you look around our culture these days, it's obvious that people are looking for simplicity, ritual, and clarity in almost every aspect of their lives. Efforts to clear the clutter from our offices, our kitchen counters, and our closets have spawned books and an entire organizational industry. So it's not surprising that the de-cluttering mindset would trickle down not only to our kitchen cabinets and refrigerators, but to our sauté pans and serving platters as well.

What does that have to do with breaking free from food obsessions? More than many of us realize. When our lives are complicated and cluttered up with stuff—material, emotional, spiritual—we tend to seek refuge in something easy and comforting, and for many of us, that "something" is food. They don't call it comfort food by chance.

We walk into our homes and see a kitchen counter piled with bills, a dishwasher that needs unloading, a refrigerator so crowded we can't see the forest for the trees, or in this case the salad for the peas. And what do we do? Throw our hands in the air, walk over to the pantry, and grab the first thing we see—chocolate chip cookies, perhaps, or maybe a box of crackers or bag of nuts. And we stand there munching, paralyzed by what we need to do to get dinner started.

So part of learning to break that mindless eating habit is by clearing out some mental and physical space so we can think clearly about our food choices and eating environments. At our house it casts a pall over my day when I don't get the dishwasher emptied before I have to start my work. I know it means breakfast dishes will be piled in the sink until I can get to them, setting off a domino effect of disarray. There's no doubt it makes me less inclined to whip up a healthy lunch than if the sink was empty, the counters cleared, and a shiny open space awaited my cutting board. As a result, I'm much more likely to grab cold pizza from the fridge for lunch rather than steam some veggies to put on top of leftover rice or even chop and wash a quick salad.

Think about your kitchen, your counter space, your dining area. Are they cluttered with papers and piles of mail? Do you eat in the midst of the mayhem? Begin to become aware of how those surroundings influence what you eat and how you eat. Who wants to eat a slow, contemplative meal in a kitchen that looks like a tornado passed through? Sometimes learning to eat with intention starts long before we ever pick up a fork.

Again, for us Catholics, an easy way to drive this point home is to think about the way in which we eat our spiritual meal, the Eucharist. The altar isn't piled with magazines and stray papers. The bread and wine aren't brought to the table in stained plasticware left over from last week's Chinese. The priest doesn't break bread with a phone perched on his shoulder and Facebook scrolling by on a laptop.

Our Sunday meal is taken in a simple but dignified manner. The altar cloth is pressed, the vessels are worthy of company, the table is clear but for the few basics that are needed to prepare the meal. The atmosphere is one of reverence and care.

There's no reason we can't bring that same simplicity and dignity to our own mealtimes, even if we're surrounded by chatty, sometimes downright noisy, dinner partners. We can clear the table of any clutter, perhaps place a candle or some other meaningful decoration at the center, use nice dishes (even if it's not fine china), keep our conversation positive and joyful, prepare and clear the meal with a sense of reverence for what we are eating and whom we are serving.

Recently my middle child was eating lunch when she heard her little sister getting into some of her things. She began yelling from the kitchen table in mid-bite. I stopped her, reminding her that yelling while eating was like swallowing anger. It's simply not good for us. It leaves us unhappy and unsatisfied, as if the meal didn't count or wasn't good, and an hour later we're back looking for something to make us feel better.

So, you see, it's all connected. There is "unity," as Brother Victor explained earlier. A good and satisfying meal is one that feeds not only our bodies but our minds and souls as well. And when we take that truly holistic, holy, and healthy approach to eating, we begin to tame the cravings, beat back the obsessions, and reframe our food-focused thinking.

Food for Thought

1. What is a typical mealtime like at your house? Is it chaotic or calm? Do you discuss positive things or use the time to hash out problems? How can you shift to a more serene atmosphere?

2. Do you involve your partner or children in the preparation process? How can you turn mealtime into an opportunity to build community?

3. Do you have the TV or stereo on when you eat? If so, what are you hearing in the background? Think about music that might be soothing or inspiring. Would you and your family be open to some sort of spiritual reading, either before or after the meal?

4. Look around your kitchen and dining room. Is it cluttered or clear? Does it create a sense of peacefulness or anxiety in you? List ways you can bring some order to your cooking and eating space.

5. How might you incorporate the monastic ideals of balance, moderation, and rhythm into your daily meals?

6. What gets in the way of making slow, sit-down meals a priority? Think about what you can change to allow yourself the luxury of cooking a simple meal at least a few times a week and sharing it with family or friends in a reverent and dignified way.

7. Do your eating and cooking styles change according to season? If so, how? Begin to become aware of the rhythm of your day and year. Think about ways to bring the seasons into your diet and mealtime in a more direct way, through the foods you choose, the blessing you say, the environment you set.

Practice

Prepare a meal or snack totally in keeping with the seasons—natural and liturgical. If it's summer, go to a local farmers' market and buy fruits or vegetables grown in your local community. If you don't have a farmers' market or it's winter, go to your grocery store and stick to fresh foods that are in season, nothing exported from across the country or over the seas. Take note of how eating locally and seasonally changes food choices dramatically.

Come home and prepare your food in keeping with monastic traditions—simple, basic, healthy, balanced. Select some spiritual reading or music appropriate to the liturgical season. As you place your food on the table, think about the altar during Mass. Consider your utensils and bowls as sacred vessels. Whether you are eating alone or in community with family or friends, notice the parallels to the Eucharistic celebration. As you prepare, eat, and clean up, contemplate the reality that God moves among the pots and pans.

Meditation

All things in moderation.
The suggestion sounds so simple,
and yet how difficult it is
to live by that maxim in a world
where more is always seen as better.
Today we strive to find the middle ground,
a place of sanity, serenity, satisfaction.
When we approach eating with a sense of
balance and reverence and simplicity,
we find we are fed in ways that go
far beyond the food that's on our plates.

Chapter 7
Soul Food
Turning meals into meditation

Lord of all pots and pans and things . . .
Make me a saint by getting meals
And washing up the plates!
Brother Lawrence

Multitasking has been elevated to an art form in our American culture. We wear it as a badge of honor, a sign that we're motivated, hardworking, busy. And busy equals important, or so we've convinced ourselves.

Rather than take a lunch hour to leisurely eat and perhaps even go for a walk, we grab something from the cafeteria or vending machines and eat at our desks while we pound out the latest office report or memo. As we race to an evening meeting straight from work, we pull food from a paper bag as we eat and drive and talk on our phone all at once. Not a second is wasted. Even at home, as we make dinner in our own kitchens, we typically rush through the process, always looking for what's next on the agenda. While we cook, we're thinking about the eating. While we eat, we're thinking about the clean-up. While we clean, we're thinking about the laundry. We are so rarely right there in the moment, cooking when we're cooking, eating when we're eating.

My husband, Dennis, recently had a conversion to mealtime mindfulness after a few months on a popular weight management program. What started as an attempt to bring his cholesterol level down and to feel healthier in general soon became a wholesale change in perspective, a change he likened to his long-ago-kicked smoking habit.

"When I was a smoker, I would smoke in my car all the time. I wouldn't get into my car without lighting up. Now, years after quitting, I see someone in a car in front of me with a cigarette in her mouth and I feel ill, watching the smoke fill the car, imagining the smell (sometimes even smelling it through my own vents)," he told me. "Now I feel that way when I see people eating in their cars. I never thought anything of it, and used to do it myself frequently. But now that I am getting used to the idea of paying attention to what I'm putting into my body and enjoying the finite amount of food I am permitting myself on a daily basis, I have that same sense watching the person gobbling up the Big Mac or slurping down the Big Gulp as I do watching the person in the smoke-filled car.

"I imagine that for them, as it used to be for me, they probably finish off their lunch without tasting it or enjoying it at all," he explained. "I find it really enlightening. It wasn't a conscious thing on my part, but a natural change in perception as I began to better understand food's place in my life. It's only been a few months since I have made these changes in my eating habits, but already I just can't remember what possible pleasure I took from that kind of eating."

What Dennis has described is the first step toward mindful eating and, as a direct result, a healthier diet and smaller waist. We can't go from zero to sixty in a day or even a week when it comes to shifting our food-habit gears. We have to take baby steps, starting with an increasing awareness of our habits and a willingness to chip away at the ones that aren't doing us any good. Slowly, with time and commitment, we move away from the rat-race, multitasking mentality to a place where we want to give our meals and ourselves the time and attention we deserve.

Lessons from the East

Mindfulness is something that is most closely associated with Buddhist thought, and rightly so. The Eastern method of focusing so singularly on one action can turn even the most mundane meal into something akin to meditation. But Christians have long had similar approaches, from monastics eating alone in their cells to universal calls for fasting and abstinence in an effort to bring spiritual depth to everyday moments. Taken slowly, or mindfully, even eating an orange or a bowl of soup, or a small piece of dark chocolate for that matter, can take on the flavor of prayer.

So often, even when we stop to say a blessing before a meal, we're mentally preparing to spoon some pasta or potatoes onto our plates. We're not usually focused on the present moment, simply placing ourselves before our food and entering into the still, slow space where eating is done for eating's sake and not something we do simply to get to the next thing on our list.

In his book *Savor: Mindful Eating, Mindful Life*, Buddhist monk Thich Nhat Hanh stresses the importance of mindful eating in overcoming weight and food issues. When we eat slowly and with complete awareness, he explains, we begin to see our connection to the greater universe, and we begin to become more selective about what we choose to put into our bodies.

"Looking deeply at the food we eat, we see that it contains the earth, the air, the rain, the sunshine, and the hard work of farmers and all those who process, transport, and sell the food. When we eat with full awareness, we become increasingly mindful of all the elements and effort needed to make our meals a reality, and this in turn fosters our appreciation of the constant support we get from others and from nature," he writes. "Whenever we eat or drink, we can engage all our senses in the eating and drinking experience. Eating and drinking like this, we not only feed our bodies and safeguard our physical health but also nurture our feelings, our mind, and our consciousness."[1]

For most of us, even the best-case meal scenario is not an exercise in mindfulness. We tend to take a big bite of food and scoop the next bite onto our fork or spoon before we've finished chewing the first. We're usually passing plates and bowls while we eat, maybe even getting into a not-so-pleasant conversation in the midst of the meal. All of that leads to less-than-mindful eating, allowing us to consume large amounts of food without even realizing it, sometimes without even tasting it.

When we begin to pay attention to our food, really pay attention, we are forced to confront some ugly realities, like how quickly we typically eat, how often we eat while talking or arguing, how little we really enjoy what we're eating because we're multitasking. So we come back around to the cold, hard truth: If we want to enjoy our food and feel good about our bodies and our weight at the same time, we have to find a way to go against the cultural grain and slow things down to a crawl.

A study conducted by the Mindfulness-Based Eating Awareness Training program and funded by the Center for Complementary and Alternative Medicine at the National Institutes of Health showed that mindful eating is "highly effective" in helping people "radically shift" their mealtime experiences.

"The individuals in the MB-EAT program have gone from binging more than four times per week, on average, to about once a week.

When they do binge, they report that the binges are much smaller and feel less out of control," writes Jean L. Kristeller, PhD, who has been exploring the role of spirituality and meditation on eating disorders for more than twenty years. "The participants are also much less depressed and experienced a much better sense of inner balance around eating."[2]

So how did they do it? Through meditative eating practices that help people become more aware of their food urges and habits and teach them how to ground themselves in the present moment, no matter what's on their plate—literally or figuratively. One woman in the study who constantly "grazed" after a big dinner, grabbing things from the fridge and eating in front of the TV, through mindful meditations began to realize her dissatisfaction with this kind of eating.

"She allowed herself a snack later if she was hungry, but stopped eating in front of the television, realizing that she enjoyed neither the food nor the TV as much when her attention was divided," Kristeller recounted.[3]

Since the rest of us don't have access to a government-funded study, how can we set ourselves on the path of mindful eating in a frenetic world where multitasking is the gold standard? We begin by simply becoming aware of the food in front of us and whether we're even hungry. How often do we stop to consider whether we're really hungry when we reach for a box of cookies or bag of chips? And if we're not really physically hungry, what exactly are we hungry for? This question brings us back to the heart of this book: Our hunger for food is far too often a hunger for something much deeper, something profoundly life-changing that we simply haven't recognized or accepted just yet. But mindfulness will lead us to that place, if we let it.

Step by Step

The next time you are about to eat, whether it's a planned meal or an impromptu snack, stop and take note of whether you're really hungry or just looking for something to do. For me, unnecessary snacking often happens when I hit a rough patch in my writing, or when I finish one project and haven't mustered the motivation to start the next so quickly. My pantry is just one floor away, so I will often wander upstairs looking for something, anything, to take me away from my computer. Despite the fact that it's a recurring habit for me, I can tell you without question that there's nothing remotely satisfying about it. I finish whatever I'm eating and immediately regret the wasted calories. I can't tell you how many times I eat a light lunch in order to be healthier only to undo it all with a bag of "lite" cracker chips two hours later. When you start to realize that mindless snacking actually robs you of your ability to have more satisfying meals throughout the day, things begin to change. Slowly.

I will realize, for example, that the calories consumed standing at the counter snacking instead of working were the equivalent of a bowl of pasta, a dish of ice cream, a glass of red wine. Why, then, am I willing to eat unsatisfying junk when I often deny myself the things I enjoy most? Because I'm not eating to fill a true hunger but to keep me otherwise occupied and in avoidance of the stuff I should be, could be, doing.

I've developed a ten-step plan for these kinds of moments. Here it is, plain and simple:

Step 1: Become aware. Start to notice what you're eating and when; whether you're hungry; what else you might truly be craving—exercise, prayer, conversation, a long drive, a better job. It could be any number of things.

Step 2: Prep with care. If you decide you are hungry and you do want to eat, prepare your meal or snack thoughtfully. Wash and peel your fruit and vegetables with a real awareness of where the food came from. As you make a sandwich, think about the many people, plants, or animals involved in making that meal possible. Your perspective really begins to change when you focus so single-mindedly on what you're doing and when you give thanks to God for what you are about to eat and for all those people who made it possible.

Step 3: Sit down to eat. You've heard it before because it is one of the key suggestions in almost every diet plan known to man. Never eat standing up, on the go, or at the counter. It makes you feel like the food doesn't count. Sort of like eating the pizza crusts or the half of a grilled cheese sandwich your kid leaves behind. It counts. They count. It all counts. When you sit down at a table, preferably in an uncluttered space with a real plate and some modicum of peace, the food is suddenly center stage. There's no denying it.

Step 4: Say a blessing. It can be a traditional grace before meals or a spontaneous blessing. It can be one line or ten. It can be focused only on your food or it can expand to include prayers for others—those who made the food possible, those who might need your prayers that day, your family, your co-workers.

My silent and meditative breakfast has become the most powerful part of my prayer life. That might sound odd, but it's true. What started as an attempt to eat more slowly and mindfully has turned into a regular prayer practice that puts me in touch with God, with loved ones and friends who are hurting, with my family, and with myself. In fact, it's gotten so intense that sometimes my oatmeal is cool before I get to it. But I wouldn't trade it, and on the weekends, when everyone is home and my house is buzzing, I really miss those few silent moments before God and my warm bowl of cereal.

Step 5: Look at your food. I mean really look at it. One healthy-food friend says we should not only look at our food closely but decide whether we are okay with this food "becoming us." In other words, whatever you put into your body will, in one fashion or another, become you—energy, fat, muscle, nutrients teeming through your veins. Is the food in front of you worthy of that? Are you turning your body into junk or are you choosing something that will make your body stronger, healthier, happier? That's not to say we can't have an occasional splurge on something totally decadent or "bad," but the vast majority of our meals, our "normal" diet, should be made up of foods that are more natural, less processed, lower in fat, and higher in fiber. You know the diet drill. Take the basics of nutrition you can find in almost any health magazine, doctor's office, or weight management plan, but add the mindfulness element to it.

Step 6: Smell your food. Really take in the aroma of what's before you. You've probably had experiences with this kind of thing without even trying. You pierce the skin of an orange and a bright, clean burst of freshness fills your nostrils, maybe even squirts into your eye. Or you sit above a hot bowl of fresh soup and breathe in the steam filled with aromas of basil and thyme, onions and celery. Not every food is going to have that kind of heady smell, but it's worth taking note. How does that cookie smell? What about the turkey sandwich on wheat? Does it have a smell at all? Just start to notice every little thing about what you're putting into your mouth.

Step 7: Eat slowly. One bite at a time. Don't pick up the next forkful or the next slice or the next cracker until the one you have in your mouth is completely gone. Maybe even put your fork or spoon down between bites to really drive home the point. And chew. Chew. Chew. Chew. Some experts say to chew each bit at least thirty times. Imagine how slow you would be eating if you chewed every individual bite thirty times? Try it. You'll be amazed.

Step 8: Focus on your food. As you eat, try to concentrate on the taste and texture of what you're eating. Don't let your mind skip ahead to dessert or your next meal or your latest work project. That's not easy. As in any form of meditation, our mind wants to race off on its own and keep busy. Just keep bringing your thoughts back to your food. Don't stare at a TV or a magazine or the junk mail you just brought in. Just eat and contemplate this one action with intensity.

Step 9: Jot it down. As we learn to become more mindful of our eating urges and habits, it's a good idea to note when and what we're eating in our food/prayer journal. You don't have to measure or list calories or grams of fat (unless you're on a specific diet that requires you to do that for health reasons). Simply write down what you ate and about how much. If you are aware of any extenuating circumstances that prompted you to eat—fight with your spouse, problem at work, bad hair day—make a note of that too so you can begin to become aware of what triggers you to eat when you might not be hungry.

I've been keeping a notebook during the process of writing this book. I keep track of what I eat throughout the day, whether I've made time to exercise, how I'm feeling physically. If I weigh myself, I jot down the number. If I've totally overdone the eating, I note that as well, a practice that has made me very much aware of when I ignore all of my own advice and want to eat for reasons beyond hunger. The practice has definitely helped my awareness and my mindfulness, and, if you are honest in your journal, it will absolutely help with overeating. Who wants to write down that she ate an entire bag of Pirate Booty, even if it is sold in the "health food" aisle? And, if you do write it down, you can bet you'll know why you're feeling so bloated or why you've put on a few pounds when you check in a few days or weeks later.

Step 10: Finish the way you started. When you are done eating, clean up with the same care you used in preparing your meal or snack. Make it one seamless, prayerful action. Mindfully wipe the table and wash your dish or place it in the dishwasher. Keeping this attitude of awareness through the end of your meal will make it less likely you'll immediately forage through the pantry or fridge for a little something extra.

General Rule: Become a planner. If you begin to plan out your menus, meals, snacks, and trips to the grocery store with these steps in mind—especially the part about what foods are you willing to become part of you—you will automatically lean toward healthier options. No one plans to eat a half-gallon of ice cream. By thinking ahead, even planning what snacks you can bring to work or eat between arriving home and starting dinner, you'll improve your chances of making better choices and doing so in a mindful way. If you know you always get home and munch as you cook, plan to munch on something worthwhile—hummus and baby carrots, a trail mix made with dried fruit and nuts. But even with those healthy options, don't just stand and stuff. Sit and savor.

Of course, no one can eat this way at every meal, unless you happen to be a monk. But eating this way on occasion or several times a week or once a day, if you're lucky, can begin to have an impact on even your non-mindful meals. Think about my husband's comments earlier in this chapter, how becoming more aware of what he was eating began to shift his overall perspective on food. That's what we're aiming for here.

Author, blogger, and mom Lisa Hendey says that her bouts with mindless eating tend to occur when she hasn't planned properly or hasn't taken appropriate breaks for meals. "I will at times get distracted by a project and not take a break for lunch. When I finally do break, I'm exhausted and starving and I make less healthy choices in my rush to eat quickly and get back to work," she told me. "My other roadblock is not having healthy food on hand in the house—fresh produce, lean meats, healthy dairy. Frequent trips to the market are often delayed thanks to my busy work and travel schedules. When I have healthy options on hand and ready to prepare, it is far easier to make good decisions about eating."

Lisa says that as she "matures," she finds her body needs less and less food to function properly, so rather than "diet," she aims to exercise better portion control. "One cookie occasionally is fine, but ten per day isn't. A nice glass of wine shared with my spouse is a blessing, but half a bottle leads to bad decisions," she explained. "If I am truly craving a favorite food, eating a small portion is often a better solution for me than trying to do without and later overindulging."

Even with those best-laid plans, sometimes the "wheels start to fall off the cart," Lisa says, and when that happens she turns to prayer, adoration, Mass, or the Rosary, as well as a focus on liturgical seasons and periodic fasting.

"Just as the Eucharist fuels our soul and our spirit, good healthful meals fuel our bodies for the work God calls each of us to do in his kingdom. Praying before we consume a meal or when we are feeling exhausted or stressed helps to bring this 'body and soul' connection into the light," she adds. "With so many around the world struggling to simply put any meal on the table, our families should also look at the bounty with which we are blessed and truly thank God and be motivated to reach out to those in need."

Eating in the Presence of God

In *Listening Below the Noise: A Meditation on the Practice of Silence*, Anne D. LeClaire talks about her decision to extend her regular practice of spending two days each month in total silence to an entire week of silence and solitude. Although she began the trip to her summer home in Cape Cod laden down with groceries, things changed unexpectedly as she allowed herself to enter fully into the silence.

"I grew most restless at mealtimes. To eat with nothing external drawing attention felt odd. Usually when I ate alone I also watched television or read. Now I felt as if I were tasting food for the first time," she wrote.

"The store of groceries I'd carried in were barely touched, as I simplified even that aspect of my days. I discovered it was harder to gulp food when there was nothing to distract, so I ate more slowly and was satisfied with less," she continued. "I had a piece of fruit for breakfast. Or a boiled egg. Lunch and dinner were pared down, too. A salad and an ear of corn. A dish of cereal topped with fresh berries."[4]

LeClaire's original plan to eat "three hearty meals a day" fell away without her even trying or realizing at first. Her desire to fill the empty space with food began to lessen as she entered into a deeply mindful place.

For Catholics, of course, that mindful place is grounded in prayer. When we link our mindful eating to prayerfulness, it packs an even bigger wallop. Even if you can't be totally mindful at every meal, if you can say a blessing, silently if necessary, or offer up a prayer for someone, something beyond yourself and your food, the prayer helps to transform eating into something that affects not only your hunger at that moment but the greater world.

When it comes to a Christian model of the kind of mindfulness we are working toward, there's really none better than Brother Lawrence, the seventeenth-century French monk whose writings in *The Practice of the Presence of God* have become a spiritual classic and a guide for those hoping to infuse their lives with a prayerful and mindful attitude.

Brother Lawrence, who could often be found cooking for his fellow brothers, spoke of his ongoing efforts to make his time in the kitchen as profound as his time in a church:

> It was observed that in the greatest hurry of business in the kitchen he still preserved his recollection and heavenly-mindedness. He was never hasty or loitering, but did each thing in its season, with an even, uninterrupted composure and tranquility of spirit. "The time of business," said he, "does not with me differ from the time of prayer; and in the noise and clatter of my kitchen, while several persons

are at the same time calling for different things, I possess
God in as great tranquility as if I were upon my knees at
the blessed sacrament."[5]

At our house there's plenty of opportunity to practice being tranquil while "several persons are at the same time calling for different things"—help with homework, snacks, permission to watch television. You name it, and they're calling for it, and I rarely manage to remain tranquil. And yet, as we see throughout Brother Lawrence's writing, our goal as Christians is to "pray without ceasing" by becoming aware of God's presence not only when we are kneeling in church but also when we are shopping for groceries or cooking dinner for hard-to-please kids.

In his Rule, St. Benedict says that monks should "regard all utensils and goods of the monastery as sacred vessels of the altar."[6] Imagine how transforming it would be if we started to view that slow cooker insert with the caked-on grime as a sacred vessel? It seems far-fetched on first reading, I'll admit, but when you start to reflect on the idea, it makes sense. This is the vessel that holds the food we have lovingly made for our families. This is our way to nourish ourselves and those we love. Of course it's sacred, and an everyday extension of the sacredness we find around the altar during Mass.

What we often don't realize is that by learning to become more aware during mealtime, which includes preparation and clean-up, we begin to lay the groundwork for becoming more aware in general. Our mindful eating gives us a template for mindful living, something we witness in the lives of the saints and other holy men and women who set their lives to a spiritual rhythm that we so rarely claim for ourselves.

Blessed Mother Teresa of Calcutta often reminded us that we are all called to do "ordinary things with extraordinary love." St. Thérèse of Lisieux preached the same in her "little way." The medieval Carmelite mystic St. Teresa of Avila, who was often found in spiritual ecstasy even when on kitchen duty, is known to have remarked: "God walks among the pots and pipkins."

And so God does the same for us today. Whether we recognize it or not, God's spirit is moving around us not only when we are in church or in silent prayer but when we are ladling out soup, slicing a loaf of crusty bread, eating a simple yogurt, or washing out a greasy frying pan. By becoming aware of God's Spirit, by slowing down and paying attention to the tastes and sounds and smells of the food we make and eat, we infuse our meals—and by extension our hearts—with a sense of awe, a depth of prayer that cannot help but transform our mindless eating into moving meditations.

The flip side of this practice works equally well, it seems. Yes, meditative meals lead to deeper prayer at the kitchen table, but deeper prayer throughout our day also leads back to more mindfulness at mealtime without us even realizing it or consciously working toward it. In his book *Why Priests Are Happy*, author Msgr. Stephen J. Rossetti includes a section called "Obesity and Prayer," and his findings support this idea that prayer and eating are intricately linked:

> An interesting finding that surfaced in this study is the correlation between private prayer and obesity. . . . Spending time in prayer does not cause one to lose weight (unless, of course, this means one spends less time eating!). However, the results give one pause. For example, priests who do not pray daily have a mean BMI value in the obese range (30 or above). On the other hand, priests who pray more than sixty minutes a day had an average BMI in the overweight range; their mean value was a full three points lower.[7]

Msgr. Rossetti goes on to explain that further correlations in the study show that those who spend more time in prayer are better able to cope with stress and rely less on food or alcohol to help them cope, and, similarly, those who said they spent more time in private prayer were less depressed and, again, less likely to turn to food as a comfort. He concludes:

> The benefits of prayer are manifold. One of the benefits of prayer appears to be an ability to deal better with stress. Prayer is also connected to a reduction in depression. Some react to depression by trying to "medicate" it through eating. These dynamics can help to explain the significant correlation between private prayer and the BMI. Priests who do not pray privately are more likely to be obese, and those who engage in a daily regimen of substantive time in prayer are likely to have a lower Body Mass Index. Prayer is good for your physical health as well.[8]

Prayer, it turns out, is a two-way street, especially when it comes to physical well-being and diet. When we eat our meals more slowly, we are more inclined to do so prayerfully, and when we pray at other points during our day, we are less inclined to eat for the wrong reasons.

Think about your own life. When you are praying regularly, just as when you are exercising regularly, do you feel more satisfied and less stressed? And yet when our lives get stressed and harried, prayer and exercise are often the first things to go. They seem like luxuries, like time wasters, but as Msgr. Rossetti and so many other experts show us, they are critical not only to our physical health but to our spiritual, mental, and emotional health as well.

Make daily prayer non-negotiable in your daily life. Don't toss it aside when you get too busy or stressed; that's when you most need it. Some experts suggest making an appointment with yourself, just as you would with your doctor or a business client, so that you clear regular space on your calendar. If that works, then by all means, use it. Find a way to make prayer as central to your life as working, as eating, as breathing.

Food for Thought

1. When you eat alone, what do you typically do? Do you watch TV or read, keep your laptop or iPhone nearby, look for "distractions"?

2. Try to remember times when you ate something while multi-tasking. Have you ever reached the end of a meal or snack and realized you don't remember eating it at all?

3. Do you tend to eat quickly or slowly? Have you ever tried to consciously slow down your eating? How did that feel? Did you get fuller faster or stop eating sooner than you otherwise might?

4. Try eating a meal or snack based on the ten steps outlined in this chapter. How did that change your experience of eating? Think about ways you might incorporate mindful eating into your schedule now and then.

5. Do you plan out your daily and weekly meals? If not, try doing so for at least one week. Plan out possible snacks as well and then go shopping for the foods you need. Skip the extras you don't need. At the end of the week, make a note of how planning changed your eating habits, if it changed them at all.

6. Review your food/prayer journal. Do you notice any places where it's obvious food is being used as a salve for stress, sadness, or other issues you're confronting in your life?

7. Think about your kitchen. Are there particular bowls or serving items that have special meaning to you, things that carry a sense

of peacefulness or sacredness about them? Begin to see these things and the other utensils you use for cooking and eating as "sacred vessels." By connecting our daily meals in concrete ways to our spiritual meal in the Eucharist, we begin to attach deeper significance to the more mundane aspects of meal preparation and eating.

8. Not every meal can be meditative. Most meals, in fact, will lean toward noisy or busy rather than calm and quiet. What are some ways you can work small elements of mindfulness into even chaotic eating situations in order to bring a level of sanity and serenity to your table?

9. If you have a fairly regular private prayer practice, begin to take note of how you feel physically on the days you pray and the days you don't. Are you more likely to eat mindlessly if you've skipped your prayer time? Why and when do you tend to skip private prayer?

Practice

Find a time when you know you will have some solitude and silence, and eat a meditative meal. Slowly and mindfully prepare your food. Do one thing at a time. Don't check email, answer the phone, read the newspaper, or watch TV. Set your place as you would for a special guest. Light a candle. Use a cloth napkin and your favorite mug or dish. Make the environment peaceful, uncluttered, and serene.

When your meal is ready, sit down and look at your food closely. Really look at it. Breathe deep and smell it, taking in all the wonderful aromas. Make the Sign of the Cross and begin to pray over your food, first for the blessing of what you have before you, for the gift of the day, your life, your home, whatever you want to express gratitude for. If there are people who need your prayers, pray for them and their intentions.

Begin to eat. Slowly. Put your fork or spoon down between bites. Do not pick up the next bite until you've finished chewing. Chew slowly and thoroughly. Think about the taste of the food you're eating. Don't think about work or cleaning or phone calls you need to make. Concentrate completely on that one bite in your mouth. When your mind starts to wander, let the thoughts float by and call yourself back to your food.

When your meal is done, slowly and quietly get up from your place. Carefully and lovingly put things away, wash your plate or bowl, wipe the table, blow out the candle, and feel the echo of this silent meal in your heart and soul.

Throughout the day, when you feel yourself getting stressed or want to grab a quick and mindless snack, think back to your meditative meal and try to recapture some of what you were feeling. If at first the exercise feels forced, keep practicing whenever you can. Before you know it, mindful meals will become a favorite practice. If you're especially daring, try a silent meal with your family, spouse, or friends one night, and see how the dynamics change.

Meditation

A space apart,
how we crave a little time,
a little solitude, a little silence
to hear ourselves think,
to pray, to live with intention.
No one will give us that space
unless we claim it for our own.

We begin with our meals,
slices of mindfulness that
become moving meditations
with every bite we take.
When we slow ourselves down,
we taste our food as if
for the first time, and suddenly
we are satisfied.

Chapter 8
Just Desserts
You can have your cake
and spiritual life, too

Man does not live on bread alone
but on every word that comes from the mouth of the Lord.
Deuteronomy 8:3

When I was on retreat at the Cistercian Abbey of the Genesee near Rochester, New York, the long and beautiful morning walk up the hill from the guesthouse to the monastery for prayer was elevated to a near-transcendent experience thanks to the smell of freshly baked bread wafting from the monastery enclosure.

As if the lush garden paths and endless cornfields under a bright blue summer sky weren't enough, the heady yeasty aroma gave a scent to my prayerful whisperings and reminded me that these silent, holy Trappist monks have made food—in this case, the production of "Monk's Bread"—part of the daily monastic rhythm that rules their lives: pray and work, *ora et labora*.

On the Saturday of my retreat, the monks had just finished baking and packing twenty-six thousand loaves. I did my part and took home as many loaves as I thought I could get away with—thirteen, I think—in every flavor and variety they offered. I rounded out my order with boxes of monk-made oatmeal and chocolate chip cookies for my kids. Lining the shelves next to the bread were food products made by Trappist monks from other communities—jams from St. Joseph's Abbey in Spencer, Massachusetts; honey from Holy Cross Abbey in Berryville, Virginia; candy from the Trappistine Sisters at Our Lady of the Mississippi in Dubuque, Iowa.

The monastic penchant for making good food isn't restricted to the Trappists. Closer to home, I can stop by my neighborhood market and pick up dense and delicious cheesecake from the Nuns of New Skete, an Eastern Orthodox monastery in the Adirondack Mountains. Brother Victor, who shared his insights on the spirituality of food in chapter 6, is famous for his flavored gourmet vinegars, touted by local foodies and chefs and featured in the *New York Times*. The Trappists of Gethsemani, the abbey Thomas Merton called home, are famous for their bourbon-laced fruitcakes and fudge as well as aged cheeses.

What's the point of sharing this menu of monastery offerings? I think it serves as a stark reminder that this spiritual journey does not require us to leave behind all the delights of this world. When we live life in balance—bringing prayer, moderation, and mindfulness into our cooking, our eating, and other aspects of our busy lives—we discover what the monastics and other holy men and women have long known: Whether we are feasting or fasting or somewhere in between, food should have a sacred role in our lives. It can be something we sacrifice, something we savor, something we share, and through it all we can remain fulfilled because we are grounded in God, the only One who can satisfy our hungry hearts.

We may need to monitor our food intake on occasion to ensure our health is good and our cholesterol low. We may opt to shed a few pounds in order to feel more comfortable in our clothes and in our own skin. We may choose to fast now and then, or even give up certain foods for good in an effort to help ourselves and others and our planet. But underneath all those possibilities will be an unshakable foundation built on love of God, moderation in all things, and compassion for ourselves and others. With that strength at our core, eating takes its rightful place and we are free to celebrate our lives with food and faith and friends in a powerful mix that reminds us over and over that we are not defined by the number on our scale but by the quality of our relationships, by our outlook, and by the blessings we begin to recognize in the everyday moments of our lives.

That doesn't mean we won't ever veer off course or backslide. Even the most devoted health and spiritual gurus aren't perfect. We just have to keep getting back up and correcting course, always looking to those in our faith life who best know how to live a balance of prayer and work, body and soul.

"Learning balance is a lifelong endeavor. One has to find personal ways to achieve balance through living in the present moment, being mindful," says Sister Evelyn Dettling, a Benedictine Sister of Pittsburgh who lives according to the Rule of St. Benedict and served as sub-prioress of her community for ten years. "Food and eating often mask our pain, our inner longing for God, for acceptance. It is key to know our motivation for eating as well as for other actions. Why do I eat? Am I tired, am I bored, am I stressed and tired? A good practice is to live in the present moment, aware of the reality in which I am immersed."

For Sister Evelyn and the other Benedictine Sisters in her community, regularly shared meals are a critical element of their spirituality, their ministry, and their overall health.

"It is a long-standing tradition that sharing the common meal together is an extension of the Eucharist. It is to provide nourishment for body and spirit," she explains. "The common table is a place of reverence for one another. Each is to anticipate the needs of the other. Everyone looks out for the needs of those who are not able bodied. It's a special time to share conversation, which is, of course, essential to building community."

At the Pittsburgh monastery, the younger Sisters learn balanced living by watching their elders. Those Sisters with weight problems have created a community-within-a-community and meet regularly over breakfast. No one has to go it alone.

"They support each other with prayer, and they share ideas about how to deal with frustration and loneliness. Some of them have devised personal physical gestures that help them let go of a difficulty or visualize handing it over to God," she told me. "They share these, they share ideas about managing food when you do not have the ability to decide or plan the menus for a week."

Sister Evelyn offered some suggestions for those of us trying to bring a spiritual rhythm and healthy balance to busy lives lived out in the world. First, create a community, either within your family or among friends. "Be open to one another. Encourage each other to see the areas of your life that are out of sync. Be aware of the treasure of pacing yourself. Do not compare yourself to someone else, and be passionately in love with God," she said, suggesting that those who face food or weight issues find a practice that can replace the mindless eating or obsessing.

"Knitting, cooking, baking, journaling, biking, walking, swimming—they all allow you to unwind, relax, and become centered," she explained, adding, "Value the sense of the divine indwelling of the Holy Spirit, and find ways to stay connected to the Divine Presence."

Creating Food Rituals

Keeping our connection to the Divine Presence, especially during mealtime, requires a little extra effort on our part. As we've discussed throughout this book, mindfulness and meditative meals don't just happen. We have to slow down, become aware, and do each thing with intention. But there are some tricks that can help us maintain that connection even when we are caught up in the craziness of life-as-usual.

We can take our cues from the practices of our own faith and those of other faiths as well. There is wisdom to be found in the rituals and rites that often accompany sacred meals and other events. By borrowing from those practices and adapting them to our own lives, we can infuse our daily lives with sacred rituals that will constantly call us back to the divine living within us and moving around us, whether we are in church or around the kitchen table.

In her book *Everyday Sacred: A Woman's Journey Home*, Sue Bender writes about her daily ritual of going to a little café to make her "to do" list for the day and write. Her cappuccino is made slowly and attentively by Martin, who always stops before he's about to hand over each drink to a customer and adds a smiling face to the foam.

"That gesture is the opening ceremony of my day," Bender writes. "Being greeted by a different smiling face each day has become a *sacred* ritual. Martin is shy, and in this situation I am also shy. We hardly talk, but his act of generosity blesses my day."[1]

When my husband and I were first married and living in the Bronx, we would head to George's Diner after church each Sunday morning. Within minutes of sitting down, our cups of hot coffee arrived and the waitress would simply confirm what she already knew: two eggs over medium, rye toast, dry—for both of us. In the hustle and bustle of a big city, we had created a ritual that made our neighborhood feel like a small town, something that was repeated when we'd stop into the Italian deli for smoked mozzarella or the bakery for fresh linguini. Even near our jobs at the Catholic Center on the East Side of Manhattan, the waitress at the nearby Chinese restaurant knew our regular order without asking.

The repetition of these small moments in our lives created rituals that brought a depth to our meals together. The eggs seemed to taste better, the cheese seemed creamier, the pasta cooked to perfection, the bean curd soup especially comforting. All these years later, those little rituals stand out as times when the sacred entered into our meals in the most unlikely ways. I think it was because the meal was about community and about relationship. The food wasn't just food; it came from hands we recognized, from people who came to know us, and it was shared between a man and a woman starting out on the road of married life together. It was a powerful combination.

Michelle Francl-Donnay, the chemistry teacher, mom, and spiritual writer we met in chapter 6, shared her own experience with ritual and sacred practice:

> My delightful and ever-patient spiritual director, Bill Sneck, S.J., thinks that we need physical ways to help us grasp the reality of being so loved by God. Hence a box of treats offered to those who come for shriving (confession) or for spiritual direction. He directly links it to the line from Psalm 34: "Taste and see the goodness of the Lord."

Michelle, or her son Chris, will often bake chocolate chip cookies for Father Bill's treat box. Once, when her niece was visiting, Michelle was stashing away the empty box that Father Bill had returned. She asked Michelle what it was, and Chris explained how Father Bill gives treats to those who come for confession.

"Her mother, overhearing this, was quick to set expectations in order, 'Don't expect anyone else to do that!' But why shouldn't we find ways to make tangible the graces of the sacraments?" Michelle wondered. "Whether they are a box of treats, or simply a welcoming word in the confessional or a joyous dismissal at the end of Mass? We are loved and this is a wonderful thing, worth exploring in all its dimensions."

Although you shouldn't expect your parish priest to offer you chocolate after absolution the next time you go to confession, you can create rituals of your own to serve as constant reminders that we are called to "taste and see the goodness of the Lord."

When we slow our actions down and begin to pay attention to the little details all along the way, we are able to turn habit into ritual, creating an aura of sacredness that seeps down into our souls. Earlier I talked about my preference for a pot of tea when I need to bring some serenity to a crazy afternoon. Despite the fact that I am a coffee lover extraordinaire, there is something about tea that changes the dynamics of my day. I don't think there's any coincidence that my calming drink of choice is the same beverage that serves as the centerpiece of the Japanese tea ceremonies that grew out of Zen Buddhism. An entire spiritual and cultural ritual is focused on tea—the making, the pouring, the serving, the surroundings, even the position of the utensils.

Susan Stabile, a law professor, retreat director, spiritual director, wife, and mom living in Minneapolis, has had firsthand experience with Japanese tea ceremonies and told me that the ritual is "at a minimum" an experience in mindfulness, but that there's also a sacredness to it due, in part, to the "simplicity of the product combined with the elaborateness and beauty of the process."

"The idea of taking this simple item—tea—that we drink every day and using it for this symbolic ritual is powerful," she said. "Of course, it's not just preparing and serving tea the way a westerner might think of it. We're not talking about plopping a teabag in a cup or even just putting some leaves in a metal basket and pouring water on it. There are special bowls used, a kind of whisk that gently stirs the powdered tea into the water," says Susan, who spent twenty years as a Buddhist before returning to her Catholic faith, some of that time living in Buddhist monasteries and retreat centers.

"Where I have participated in tea ceremonies, it has been in a small area near a fresh water source. It is usual to bow as one enters. There is very simple décor so that nothing detracts from the attention on the process," she continues. "All of the movements are very slow and deliberate, and there are no extra movements."

Although she doesn't practice any specific rituals with food or drink now, Susan believes that her experience infused elements of her cooking and eating with a sense of the sacred. Chopping vegetables, in particular, is meditative for her, as she told me just a day after returning from a weekend retreat.

"The retreat I just gave was a silent one. After the retreat, one of the participants came up to me and said that she was glad she sat next to me during the silent meals because I ate so mindfully and it was a good example to her," she added.

While most of us may never experience a true Japanese tea ceremony, we probably have habits that lend themselves to creating sacred rituals with simple ingredients—the twelve almonds we shake from the container to mix in a small glass bowl with dried cranberries for a mid-morning snack, the low-fat biscotti we unwrap and gingerly dip into our afternoon coffee, the Friday night pizza we roll out on the kitchen counter as we sip a glass of wine. On the surface they may seem rather pedestrian compared to the stark beauty of a tea ceremony, and yet, when we take those existing habits and infuse them with attention to details and with gratitude to God, we create something special, something that feeds more than our stomachs.

When I allow my kids to join in the pizza making at our house, it becomes an event. Maybe not the most peaceful of moments, what with all the flour and cheese being tossed about, but a time verging on sacred because it combines homemade food lovingly made, my own little family community, the warmth of our home, and the joy of eating a favorite meal together. The kids roll out the dough, spread the sauce, sprinkle on cheese, and carefully place mushrooms or olives or peppers on top of their individual pizzas, so pleased with their culinary handiwork. They peer through the glass oven door to see how it's cooking and wait with anticipation for it to cool enough for cutting. They have special pizza pans, special rolling pins, special aprons. Seeing the smiles on their flour-smudged faces touches my heart, makes me grateful, extends my patience, and brings all of us a small modicum of extra grace.

It's a whole different experience from the nights when we pick up pizza to go in a cardboard box and serve it lukewarm on paper plates. Little things can shift a moment from habit to ritual, from mundane to meaningful. You can look at your life and begin to give a little more depth and weight to the things that seem ready-made for this.

Even if you can't think of one existing habit-ritual in your life right now, it's easy to develop one surrounding a favorite food or drink, a favorite restaurant, a favorite family meal, or a favorite time of day. We've already established that my silent breakfast ritual is a must for me, something that has transformed at least one meal a day into a prayer and has made me less likely to feel unsatisfied when I'm finished. When I'm at the dinner table and things are getting noisy or tense, I find myself taking a deep breath, looking down at my dinner plate, reminding the kids that we shouldn't eat in such a way, and then consciously slowing down my eating and my thoughts. I believe it's only possible for me to do that because I have my experience with the slow, sacred ritual of silent breakfast.

The rituals we create ripple outward and touch others, first in our own home and then in the world outside. Think about Father Bill and the little chocolate treat offered to Michelle, who then goes home and tells her son, who offers to bake more treats and tells her niece about the practice. Who knows where the ripples stop? When we link our eating and our prayer and begin to see food as part of a much bigger picture, rather than the focal point of our entire lives, we reshape the way we think, the way we act, and the way we interact.

Feeding Hearts and Souls

You may have noticed by now an undercurrent of community running through our conversation on balance, ritual, and mindfulness. We are not meant to walk this journey alone. Jesus sent his disciples out in pairs so they would have much-needed companionship for the journey ahead. And so it is for those of us traversing the often-frustrating path of sane eating habits, healthy self-image, and moderation in all things. We need companions, community.

Too often, especially among women, there is a sense of competition rather than community when it comes to diet and weight loss. We don't want to admit that we're unhappy with ourselves and so we try to achieve our goals in a bubble. But community is critical to our physical, spiritual, and mental health, which explains, in part, the success of certain popular diet programs. The community support, the element of accountability, the friends who share similar struggles all come together to provide the encouragement and direction we can't get flying solo.

We've talked a lot about family meals, and that's critical for building real community among parents and children. But it's also important for adults to have a sense of community with peers, especially those walking a similar path. Look for friends, in particular spiritual friends, who share not only your desire to find a place of peace when it comes to food and body image, but who also share your hunger for a deeper relationship with God. Through regular conversations, occasional get-togethers, and constant feedback via email, phone, Facebook, or whatever means works best, you can build your own support system and community.

Our faith has a long history of food-related rituals grounded in community, and we can build on that foundation. Our Jewish ancestors understood the potential for spiritual transformation through physical meals when shared among people of faith. Chanukah, Rosh Hashanah, Sukkot, Purim, and Passover all have specific foods and feasts connected to spiritual events and celebrations. We see evidence of this deep understanding of the communal meal in Jesus' own life. In the Gospel stories, Jesus is seen repeatedly dining with both the powerful and the downtrodden, turning water into wine at a wedding feast, multiplying loaves and fishes for a hungry crowd, celebrating a Passover meal that would be unlike any other before or after.

We can use the Eucharistic meal as a touchstone when we are trying to build community and create rituals in our own lives. By recalling that beautiful, slow-moving, mindful celebration of faith, we can begin to draw the parallels and bring similar elements into our physical lives.

David M. Thomas, author of *A Community of Love: Spirituality of Family Life*, writes that the communal feast, as was celebrated regularly among the earliest Christians even in the face of persecution, remains as "an ideal and as an expression of our basic oneness before God."

"The family meal is a special way of celebrating the presence of God in our midst. It is an opportunity for prayer and play. It is a place where family life can reach a certain crescendo of intensity," writes Thomas, who goes on to share his family's nightly ritual of "plusses and minuses," where each family member shares one positive and one negative aspect of their day.[2]

"Once everyone has filled his or her plate with food, one family member leads grace and initiates the ritual of sharing the day. . . . Then, like the passing of food, the telling of the day's events for each person begins."[3]

We tried this around our family dinner table not long after I first read about it. I wondered if my teenage son would balk or if my youngest would be stumped, but it was a really fun and somewhat enlightening way to have every person at the table offer some insights into their day and their feelings. It definitely brought a sense of the sacred to the table, even with one child offering video games as a highlight. We have also experimented with *The Meal Box*, a deck of cards with fun questions like "If you could open the back door to your house and step out into the perfect backyard, what would the yard be like?" or "If you could have one hundred of anything right now, what would you choose?"

I originally started that exercise as a review of the product for a blog, but my kids will pull the deck of cards out of the drawer pretty regularly and ask to include it in our dinner conversation. Rather than bickering over who didn't get the milk or lapsing into tense conversations about rooms not cleaned or homework undone, these kinds of conversation starters lead us into the building up of community. It could work just as well for a group of friends gathered for a Friday night meal or an extended family sharing dinner on a Sunday afternoon. Try it, and see how these kinds of conversations shift the meal away from the secular toward the sacred.

Obviously these exercises prove that keeping the connection between food and faith does not mean you have to be constantly praying before, during, and after your meals in an outward and obvious way. This is more about developing a prayerful mindset that becomes the basis of all your meals—those eaten alone, those eaten as a family or community, those eaten slowly and mindfully, and even those eaten when you hardly have time to sit and enjoy. You will find that when you begin to develop rituals, build community, and nurture gratitude, a sense of prayerfulness will work its way into even the most un-mindful meal or snack.

Even with all this attention to contemplative eating, truth be told, I will still run upstairs from my desk during the day now and then for a bite to eat when I'm really not hungry. I just need a break from my work, and I'm only human after all. Sometimes I just want to grab a bag of chips and eat right from the bag. Standing at the counter, even. And yet, I never eat that way anymore without complete awareness of what I'm doing. If I choose to eat tortilla chips standing up, you can bet the little voice inside will be reminding me that it's not a healthy or mindful way to eat. I'm likely to clip the bag and go back to my work having eaten only four or five chips where once I might have eaten four or five handfuls of chips.

Little shifts make for big differences in diet, weight, and overall attitude. When you take all that we've discussed in these pages and put them into practice one piece at a time, you set a new course for your diet and your life. So find your ritual, build your community, become more mindful, and, with God's help, begin to change your present and your future one bite at a time.

Food for Thought

1. Do you have any daily food rituals? If so, are they healthy or unhealthy? Think of ways to adjust your ritual or create a ritual that will weave a sense of the sacred into a favorite meal or snack.

2. How often do you eat in "community," either with family or friends? Do your meal conversations tend to focus on family or work issues or responsibilities? Begin to introduce practices that will shift conversation away from tension or "shoulds" and focus more on relationship and the sharing of personal stories.

3. Where might you begin to build a new community, or nurture one that may be in the early stages of developing? Is there a group of friends you could tap into to join you on your food-faith journey?

4. Contemplate the place of gratitude, not only at the start of your meals but as part of the rhythm of your day. Begin to see the blessings around you and start making a note of them. Perhaps even start a gratitude journal. When we are thankful for what we have, we tend to focus less on what we think we're missing.

5. Is there an activity you can fall back on when none of the rituals or community support or journaling is helping? Do you like to knit or bowl, walk or do yoga, garden or do crossword puzzles? When you feel yourself losing your balance, go to your fallback activity. You may need some variety. For example, if you're at work and want to go to the vending machine, you can't pick up your knitting. So find a substitute. Perhaps get up from your desk and walk around the office, or do some slow breathing exercises or a brief meditation at your desk.

6. The next time you're at Mass, focus on the details of the Eucharistic meal. Look for the parallels to your meals at home and consider ways you can weave some of those sacred elements into everyday life. Do you eat on paper plates? Do you eat straight from the container? Do you rush through your meal? Write down some ways you can adjust your mealtime habits to mimic the slow beauty of the Eucharistic feast.

7. Go back to the first exercise we did at the end of chapter 1. Have you continued the spiritual practice you began at that time? How has it impacted your eating habits and your life? If you have not continued the practice, why? Did you substitute another spiritual practice? If not, try again now to repeat that chapter 1 exercise for at least a week or two and see if it makes a difference.

8. How is your prayer life overall? Are you praying daily? Are you reading scripture? Are you getting to Mass and receiving the Eucharist? If so, have you seen a correlation between prayer and your ability to face down your food issues? If not, begin to work on your prayer life since it is critical to your physical, emotional, mental, and spiritual well-being. Write down some ways you can add more prayer to your daily routine. Watch how these practices impact your eating habits and overall satisfaction with yourself, your life, your relationship with others, and your connection to the Creator.

Practice

Create a food ritual that will permanently link food and faith in your heart and mind. Start with something small—one square of extra dark chocolate placed lovingly on a small bamboo cutting board and shared with your spouse after dinner each night as the two of you sit on the couch and share stories from your day, a cup of tea made slowly and mindfully on a Saturday afternoon and sipped in silence as you look out at the rain or snow or sunshine, a family dinner shared every Friday night to celebrate the end of the work and school week with everyone taking part in the cooking, table setting, conversation, and cleanup. Make it something that will hold meaning for you, something you'll look forward to again and again.

Once you've decided on what your ritual will be, give it all your attention. Link it with prayer. Focus on this special blessing as you eat or drink, and breathe in the beauty of this simple but powerful exercise. Let your ritual bless your day and become an opportunity to bring body, mind, and spirit together in harmony.

Meditation

When we infuse our actions
with a focus on God and on
the many blessings we receive
in even the most mundane
moments of our lives,
we create sacred rituals
that bring a sense of holiness,
a sense of wholeness,
to what we do and who we are.
Like the Eucharistic feast
that nourishes our heart and soul,
every meal we eat with mindfulness
each bite we take with gratitude,
has the power to transform us
inside and out, for all time.

Appendix:
Practices for the Journey Forward

1. A 10-Step Plan to Saner, Mindful Eating

This plan, a condensed version of what's included in chapter 7, is a handy go-to guide when you're feeling stressed and unable to cope with cravings and mindless eating.

Step 1: Become aware. Are you really hungry? What else might you be craving or facing that is making you turn to food?

Step 2: Prep with care. If you are hungry, prepare your meal or snack thoughtfully. Focus on your many blessings—where the food came from, the plants, animals, and people who made it possible, how God is moving in your life, even in your kitchen, your office, or your grocery store.

Step 3: Sit down to eat. Never eat standing up, on the go, or at the counter. It makes you feel like the food doesn't count. Sit down at a table, preferably in an uncluttered space with a real plate and some modicum of peace; make the food center stage.

Step 4: Say a blessing. It can be a traditional grace before meals or a spontaneous expression of gratitude.

Step 5: Look at your food. Decide whether you are okay with this food "becoming you."

Step 6: Smell your food. Really take in the aroma of what's before you.

Step 7: Eat slowly. One bite at a time. Don't take the next bite until the one you have in your mouth is completely gone. Chew slowly and carefully.

Step 8: Focus on your food. As you eat, concentrate on the taste and texture of your food. Don't let your mind skip ahead to dessert or your next meal or your latest work project. Just eat and contemplate this one action with intensity.

Step 9: Jot it down. In your food/prayer journal, write down when and what you're eating. Note any extenuating circumstances or problems that may have prompted you to eat when you might not be hungry.

Step 10: Finish the way you started. When you are done eating, clean up with the same care you used in preparing your meal or snack. Make it one seamless, prayerful action.

General Rule: Become a planner. If you begin to plan out your menus, meals, snacks, and trips to the grocery store with these steps in mind, you will automatically lean toward healthier options.

2. Go on Retreat

A retreat may sound like an odd suggestion for someone trying to get a handle on healthy eating, but it's actually the perfect way, the perfect place, to bring the food-faith connection to light. Most monasteries or retreat houses tend to focus on basic, healthy food. If you shop around, you'll also be able to find locations where meals are taken in silence.

Just two days devoted to prayer, relative silence, and limited, healthy eating can offer a real jumpstart on personal transformation. It's an opportunity to spend some quality time with yourself and God, unfettered by the need to cook, the temptation of the fridge, and the clamor of the outside world. If nothing else, you will come home refreshed and ready to take on the next step in this gradual move toward more mindful eating and living.

3. Grocery Store Field Trip

Food shopping is a lot like walking or driving for most of us. We tend to go on automatic pilot, throwing the usual food favorites into our carts as we bob and weave through the aisles. The next time you have to go to the market, act like a tourist. Explore regions you've never been to before, and skip the usual boring stuff.

To ensure your field trip focuses on what's healthy, hug the outer perimeter of the store. That's where the good stuff (a.k.a. nutritious food) tends to be—produce, dairy, fresh-baked breads, bulk items, lean meats. Pick up some new foods, especially if they happen to be in season at the time. Explore those bulk bins (if you're lucky enough to have them in your market) filled with whole grains, nuts, seeds, and other healthy goodies. Get to know what parts of the freezer section are healthful and what's off limits. (Frozen veggies are good. Frozen mac and cheese is not so good.)

Take a trip down the "ethnic" aisle, where you can often find exotic offerings to spice up your healthy dinners, from salsas or dried beans in the Mexican section to rice noodles in the Chinese section to chutneys in the Indian section. There are loads of other options from various cuisines that often get skipped over when we're honing in on pre-packaged rice dishes or canned soups.

Notice, as you pass through the center aisles and get some of your necessities, how the super-sugary, fat-laden convenience foods tend to be at eye level and easiest to grab. That's not where you want to spend most of your time.

Once you're done, all that's left is to get through the candy gauntlet at the check-out counter.

4. Spiritual Exercises

I'm not talking about the Ignatian Exercises here. I'm referring to a combination of physical exercise and prayer. Once you've checked with your doctor to make sure it's safe for you to start an exercise program, explore ways to weave prayer and physical activity into your life at the same time. So often when we get busy, prayer and exercise are the first things to go. We think of them as extras, luxuries, but they are both critical to a healthy, happy life.

If you don't like "formal" exercise programs, such as aerobics classes or yoga or spinning, simply start with walking. It doesn't even have to be fast walking. Just start moving. And as you move, begin to pray and breathe and focus. The spiritual and physical combination will give added strength to your efforts back home around the dinner table. It's really a win-win-win situation. You work off stress, spend time with God, lower your cholesterol, take off extra pounds, and build muscle—spiritual and physical—all at once.

5. Start a Movement

Find some friends who have the same general goals and spiritual interests and band together. Become a support system, a spiritual community. Meet regularly to talk about progress, struggles, successes, and more. Share tips for keeping food in its rightful place and prayer at the center of your meals and days.

Share a communal meal, focusing not only on the food you eat but on the preparation, the blessing, the conversation, the togetherness, the ways a regular dinner shared with friends can parallel our experience of our spiritual meal at Mass. Make it a feast for the senses, not necessarily in calories but in spirit.

6. Fasting: It's Not Just for Lent

Make some sort of fasting or abstinence a regular part of your life. Lent is the perfect time to try this spiritual practice since you'll have the support of the larger Church, but it's beneficial for body and soul when we incorporate this into ordinary life and Ordinary Time as well.

Choose one day per week or one day per month when you will institute some sort of fasting practice coupled with prayer. Perhaps eat only fruit for breakfast and clear broth for lunch, saving your one meal of the day for dinner. Give up meat one day per week if that's something you love, or your afternoon latte on certain days. But always be sure the fasting is linked to prayer or it will become just one more method of dieting. Offer your sacrifice for your family, for those you know who are ill, for those who are hungry. Every time your stomach growls or you go to reach for a piece of candy and stop yourself, say a prayer for whatever intention you've chosen.

7. Advent: A New Twist on Holiday Treats

'Tis the season to pack on a few pounds. Between Thanksgiving and New Year's Day, most of us are faced with plates of cookies and homemade candies, special fat-laden side dishes at holiday meals, and office or neighborhood parties where almost everything is on the "naughty" list.

Turn things around by joining in the baking and cooking festivities, but go one step further. Instead of loading up your own counters with cookies and peppermint bark, bake it, make it, and then give it away. It's the perfect way to bring our love of food and love of others together in one generous swoop. Head down to the home of your elderly neighbor with a tray of goodies, invite a lonely person over to share your famous sweet potato casserole, host a dessert night and invite family and friends to come over and sample what you've made with love and gratitude.

Find special recipes that tie into seasonal feasts, rather than feasting all season long. Put oranges in your kids' shoes on St. Nicholas Day, December 6; bake St. Lucy's Bread on December 13; hide a small symbol of the baby Jesus in your King Cake on the Feast of the Epiphany. There are so many beautiful food possibilities linked with the many feasts of our faith. Celebrate them!

8. Closet Clean-Out

Go through your clothes closet and bureau drawers and weed out the jeans from ten years ago that were too tight even then, the post-pregnancy dress you're keeping in case you put on more weight, the out-of-style skirt you have stashed away as the benchmark of your perfect size. Don't live your life in a perpetual state of limbo, always hoping to be thinner or expecting to be heavier.

Pare down your wardrobe to those items that fit well, make you feel good, and suit your purpose and personality. It's the quickest way to lose quite a few unwanted and unnecessary pounds, and, if you bring the clothes to Goodwill, Catholic Charities, or some other outreach ministry, you can help others at the same time.

Notes

Chapter 1: A Deeper Hunger: Filling the spiritual void with food

1. Oliver, *New and Selected Poems*, 94.

Chapter 2: Dieting Delusion: Food is not the enemy

1. Poust, *The Complete Idiot's Guide to the Catechism of the Catholic Church*, 209.

2. Ward, *The Desert Fathers*, xviii.

3. Paul VI, *Gaudium et Spes*, No. 14.

4. Kessler, *The End of Overeating*, 117–18.

5. Ibid., 117.

6. Martin, *Becoming Who You Are*, 29.

Chapter 3: Mirror, Mirror: Discovering our true selves

1. Kesten, "Create an Enlightened Diet," *Spirituality and Health Magazine: The Body and Soul Connection*, Special Issue 2012, 54.

2. Patalinghug, *Grace Before Meals*, viii.

3. Ibid., ix.

4. Benedict XVI, *God Is Love*, 8.

5. McKenna, *Not Counting Women and Children*, 17.

6. Ibid., 18.

Chapter 4: Freedom by the Forkful: Breaking the chains of a high-fat, fast-food culture

1. Bittman, *The Food Matters Cookbook*, 6.

2. Chan, "Diet Soda Linked to Weight Gain," *HuffPost Healthy Living*, August 29, 2011.

3. Bittman, *The Food Matters Cookbook*, 6.

4. Ibid., 10.

5. Talbot, *The Lessons of St. Francis*, 26.

Chapter 5: Feast or Famine: Changing attitudes toward how and why we eat

1. Steinhauer, "I'll Try My Luck," *New York Times*, December 14, 2011.

2. Dolan, "Sometimes There Is an 'Easy Answer,'" *Catholic New York*, September 23, 2010.

3. Ibid.

4. O'Connor, "The Claim: To Cut Calories, Eat Slowly," *New York Times Health*, February 22, 2010.

5. Miles, "Toward a New Asceticism," *Christian Century*, October 28, 1981, 1097–1098.

6. Ibid.

7. Huston, *The Holy Way*, 81.

Chapter 6: Balancing Act: Cues from the monastics

1. d'Avila-Latourrette, *Simplicity from a Monastery Kitchen*, x.

2. Francl-Donnay, "Soup and Psalms Measure Life's Tempo," *Catholic Standard & Times*, February 11, 2010.

Chapter 7: Soul Food: Turning meals into meditation

1. Nhat Hanh, *Savor*, 97–98.

2. Kristeller, "How to Make Every Bite a Spiritual Experience," *Spirituality and Health Magazine: The Soul-Body Connection*, Special Issue 2012, 59.

3. Ibid., 61.

4. LeClaire, *Listening Below the Noise*, 163.

5. Brother Lawrence, *The Practice of the Presence of God*, 30.

6. *Rule of St. Benedict*, 31:10.

7. Rossetti, *Why Priests Are Happy*, 33.

8. Ibid., 34–35.

Chapter 8: Just Desserts: You can have your cake and spiritual life, too

1. Bender, *Everyday Sacred*, 38.

2. Thomas, *A Community of Love*, 56.

3. Ibid., 59.

Bibliography

Bender, Sue. *Everyday Sacred: A Woman's Journey Home*. San Francisco: Harper One, 1995.

Benedict of Nursia. *The Rule of St. Benedict*. New York: Image Books, 1975.

Benedict XVI. *Deus Caritas Est*. Washington, DC: USCCB, 2006.

Bittman, Mark. *The Food Matters Cookbook*. New York: Simon & Schuster, 2010.

Brother Lawrence. *The Practice of the Presence of God with Spiritual Maxims*. Grand Rapids, MI: Spire Books, 1958.

Catechism of the Catholic Church. 2nd ed. Washington, DC: USCCB, 1994, 1997.

Chan, Amanda. "Diet Soda Linked to Weight Gain." *HuffPost Healthy Living*. August 29, 2011.

d'Avila-Latourrette, Victor-Antoine. *Simplicity from a Monastery Kitchen*. New York: Broadway Books, 2001.

Dolan, Timothy. "Sometimes There Is an 'Easy Answer.'" Lord, to Whom Shall We Go. *Catholic New York*. September 23, 2010.

Francl-Donnay, Michelle. "Soup and Psalms Measure Life's Tempo." *Catholic Standard & Times*. February 11, 2010.

Huston, Paula. *The Holy Way: Practices for a Simple Life*. Chicago: Loyola Press, 2003.

Kessler, David A. *The End of Overeating: Taking Control of the Insatiable American Appetite*. Large print ed. Detroit: Thorndike Press, 2009.

Kesten, Deborah. "Create an Enlightened Diet." *The Soul Body Connection: 2012 Guide to Spirituality & Health*. Special Issue 2012.

Lamott, Anne. *Traveling Mercies: Some Thoughts on Faith*. New York: Pantheon Books, 1999.

LeClaire, Anne D. *Listening Below the Noise: A Meditation on the Practice of Silence*. New York: HarperCollins, 2009.

Martin, James, S.J. *Becoming Who You Are: Insights on the True Self from Thomas Merton and Other Saints*. Mahwah, NJ: Hidden Spring, 2006.

Miles, Margaret. "Toward a New Asceticism." *Christian Century*. October 28, 1981.

McKenna, Megan. *Not Counting Women and Children: Neglected Stories from the Bible*. Maryknoll, NY: Orbis Books, 1994.

Nhat Hanh, Thich, and Dr. Lilian Cheung. *Savor: Mindful Eating, Mindful Life*. New York: Harper One, 2010.

Nicholaus, Bret, and Tom McGrath. *The Meal Box*. Chicago: Loyola Press, 2009.

O'Connor, Anahad. "The Claim: To Cut Calories, Eat Slowly." *New York Times*. February 22, 2010.

Oliver, Mary. *New and Selected Poems*. Boston: Beacon Press, 1992.

Patalinghug, Father Leo. *Grace Before Meals: Recipes for Family Life*. Hunt Valley, MD: Leo McWatkins Film, Inc., 2009.

Pollan, Michael. *In Defense of Food: An Eater's Manifesto*. New York: Penguin, 2009.

Paul VI, *Gaudium et Spes (The Pastoral Constitution of the Church in the Modern World)*. 1965.

Poust, Mary DeTurris. *The Complete Idiot's Guide to the Catholic Catechism*. New York: Alpha/Penguin USA, 2008.

Rossetti, Stephen J. *Why Priests Are Happy: A Study of the Psychological and Spiritual Health of Priests*. Notre Dame, IN: Ave Maria Press, 2011.

Ryan, Thomas, C.S.P., ed. *Reclaiming the Body in Christian Spirituality*. New York/Mahwah, NJ: Paulist Press, 2004.

Steinhauer, Jennifer. "I'll Try My Luck: 'Store bought' spoils the potluck spirit." *New York Times*. December 14, 2011.

Talbot, John Michael, and Steve Rabey. *The Lessons of St. Francis: How to Bring Simplicity and Spirituality into Your Daily Life.* New York: Plume/Penguin, 1998.

Thomas, David M. *A Community of Love: Spirituality of Family Life.* Skokie, IL: ACTA Publications, 2007.

Ward, Benedicta. *The Desert Fathers: Sayings of the Early Christian Monks.* New York: Penguin, 2003.

Williamson, Marianne. *A Return to Love: Reflections on the Principles of A Course in Miracles.* New York: HarperCollins, 1992.

Mary DeTurris Poust is an author, columnist, journalist, speaker, and blogger who has written for dozens of Catholic and secular publications. She is the author of *Walking Together, Everyday Divine, The Complete Idiot's Guide to the Catholic Catechism*, and *Parenting a Grieving Child*. Poust was a senior correspondent and contributing editor for *Our Sunday Visitor* newspaper for fourteen years and is a daily contributor to *Our Sunday Visitor's* popular blog, *OSV Daily Take*. Her award-winning monthly column "Life Lines" has been published in *Catholic New York* since 2001. Poust also writes about family, faith, and the spiritual journey at her own blog, *Not Strictly Spiritual*. She has worked for the dioceses of Metuchen, New Jersey, and Austin, Texas, as well as the Archdiocese of New York, where she served as managing editor of *Catholic New York*. She lives in upstate New York with her husband and three children.